LISTEN TO THE HEART

LISTEN TO THE HEART

Creating
Intimate Families
Through the Power of
Unconditional Love

Roberta Meyer

WARNER BOOKS

A Warner Communications Company

Warner Books, Inc., 666 Fifth Avenue, New York, NY 10103

W A Warner Communications Company

Book Design by Nick Mazzella.

Printed in the United States of America

First printing: June 1989

10 9 8 7 6 5 4 3 2

Library of Congress Cataloging-in-Publication Data

Meyer, Roberta.
    Listen to the heart : creating intimate families through the power
of unconditional love / by Roberta Meyer.
        p.   208
    ISBN 0-446-51432-2
    1. Family.   2. Communication in the family.   3. Intimacy
(Psychology)   I. Title.
HQ518.M48   1989
306.8′5—dc19   88-37296
                                                                          CIP

DEDICATION

To all my "FAMILIES"—you know who you are

Acknowledgments

That I should be writing about intimacy is nothing short of a miracle. Intimacy absolutely requires the ability to hear feedback, which to someone like myself means *criticism*.

Feedback or criticism, constructive or otherwise, was not something I could tolerate for the first 27 years of my life. But at the age of 27 something occurred that forced me to take an honest look at myself. I had made my third suicide attempt and was down for the count. Fortunately, I received some feedback which changed my entire life. I began to explore issues of addiction, communication, self-knowledge, and intimacy and much of what I learned is discussed in this book.

My teachers along the way have been numerous, and I would like to acknowledge them.

Bill W. and Dr. Bob showed me the way to sobriety. Lois W. taught me about detachment with love. Earl Marsh helped me discover that feelings were OK, and Werner Erhard taught me that they needn't be my master.

In self-actualizing seminars I learned from Stewart Emery that excellence and love could co-exist. My husband, Bill, and daughters, Megan and Deborah Ann taught me that I was truly lovable, regardless of my peculiarities.

My mother, Virginia, and sister, Priscilla allowed me to practice my theories of family intimacy on them, as have the many friends who make up my "chosen" family.

I have learned most, however, from my clients, who with courage and trust have gone into the world armed with the hypotheses in this book and demonstrated their validity.

The book could never have been written without the support and expertise of my colleague, Carol Costello. And my editor, Joann Davis, has been not only helpful, but extremely patient with my queries.

To all of you I say thank you for your participation in this book and in my life.

Contents

PREFACE: Making a Contribution   1

CHAPTER ONE: A Fresh Start   5
    What Intimacy Is *Not*
    What Intimacy Is
    Whom Do You Trust?
    Why We Crave Intimacy
    Robot and Spirit
    Conscious Choice
    Risk and Support
    The Intimate Family

CHAPTER TWO: The Changing Family   33
    The Family and Intimacy
    Family Roles
    Family Dynamics
    The Dysfunctional Family

CHAPTER THREE: Intimacy by Choice 61
Intimacy Can't Be Forced
The First Step
Intimacy Begins Unilaterally—or, "You Go First"
Choices
Letting Go of Barriers
Is It Worth It?

CHAPTER FOUR: Intimate Communication 77
Robot or Spirit?
Addiction to Nonintimate Communication
Guidelines for Intimate Communication
    1. Watch out for "stuffing" and "dumping."
    2. Don't justify your responses.
    3. Be aware of payoffs and hidden agendas.
    4. Listen to yourself.
    5. Let go of the need to be "right" and to win at another's expense.
    6. Practice moccasin walking.
    7. Don't be afraid to use outside resources.

CHAPTER FIVE: Where Intimacy Breaks Down 95
    1. Expectations
    2. Fear of loss
    3. Communication from the Robot rather than Spirit
    4. Holding on to the past
    5. Resentments
    6. Trying to change others
    7. You can't ever get enough of what you don't want
    8. Needing to be needed
    9. The idea that love is something we have to earn
    10. The idea that others are doing less than they are capable of doing

11. The idea that people are not communicating
     when in fact they are

CHAPTER SIX: Intimacy in Your Biological Family   123
     Choosing Your Biological Family
     1. Examine your expectations.
     2. Accept that this is how it is in your family and
         that this is probably how it's going to be.
     3. Given that this is how it is, what can you do to
         fulfill your own needs?
     4. Be willing to create a life for yourself in this
         context.
     5. Discover your family's common bonds and
         interests, and capitalize on them.
     6. Choose whether or not you want to create
         intimacy within your own biological family.
     Committing to Intimacy in Your Biological Family
     1. Clean the slate.
     2. Tell the truth, even when it's risky.
     3. Be willing to keep hearing the truth.
     4. Communicate directly.
     5. Remember that everything communicates, all
         the time.
     6. Recognize that intimacy is a state you live in,
         not something you do every now and then.
     7. Encourage those around you to follow these
         steps.
     8. Be descriptive, not evaluative.
     9. Keep communications current.

CHAPTER SEVEN: How to Create a "Chosen" Family   143
     Why Create a New Family?
     1. Your biological family is no longer living.

2. You have been "divorced" from your biological family.
3. The relationship with your biological family is intact but not intimate.
4. You simply want to expand the quality and quantity of intimacy in your life.

Reaching Out

Choosing People

Creating Your Own Family

1. Tell yourself the truth about the fact that you have no family.
2. Let go.
3. Recognize that there are still lessons to be learned.
4. Clean the slate with your biological family.
5. Take some time off to enjoy your freedom.
6. Explore what "family" really means to you.
7. Create your new family out of common bonds, interests, and commitments.
8. Stick your neck out.
9. Create a history with your new family.

Co-Workers Are Not Family

The Reward

CHAPTER EIGHT: Special Families   163
    Step Families
    Gay Families
    Single-Parent Families
    Families With Two Working Parents
    Families With an Illness
    If Your Family Is Dysfunctional

CHAPTER NINE: Choosing Intimacy   179
    The Choice *Not* to Be Intimate
    Why Choose Intimacy?

LISTEN
TO THE
HEART

MAKING A CONTRIBUTION

Intimacy. Family. Two volatile words, especially when they appear together, especially now.

They are supposed to be concepts that make us happy and give meaning to our lives. But sometimes our experiences with family and intimacy produce as much sadness, guilt, and anger as they do love, exhilaration, and joy. I know this is the case because during the past fifteen years as a family mediator, addiction and communication consultant, and seminar leader, I have worked with more than four thousand people troubled by issues involving communication and intimacy. As a consultant to businesses, nonprofit corporations, families, and individuals I have responded to questions that are fundamentally the same. What is intimacy? When is it appropriate to be intimate? Does the concept have something to do with sex? Can it be shared with more than a few people? And what is family? Is it a group comprised only of blood relatives? What about my in-laws? What if I can't stand them?

One reason for the confusion is that our ideas about both intimacy and family are changing quickly and dramatically. The old pictures of "intimacy"—people snuggled comfortably around a fire, people who are always loving and generous, people who never speak harsh or impatient words—are a romantic vision at best. We know life isn't always like that, but we also know there is *something* about those pictures that we want. We have begun looking for new ways of relating to others—family, friends, and lovers—that are realistic, but that also give depth and meaning to our lives.

At the same time, our notions of what "family" means are profoundly different from what they were even ten or twenty years ago. The white picket fence, the mom and dad with 2.5 children and a dog have given way to new and broader definitions of family that are exciting and full of potential, but can also be disquieting.

In my work with clients recovering from the physical and emotional ravages of addiction; as an educator to children requiring special skills to deal with an alcoholic parent; as a counselor to couples attempting to resolve the pain of an extramarital affair; as a victim of family conflicts arising from my own alcoholism and recovery, I see why many of us feel as if we've somehow slipped through the crack between the old and the new. We know that the old images and definitions of an intimate family don't work particularly well, but we're not quite sure yet what the new ones are, or if they're going to serve us any better. Many of us feel that something in our experience is missing, something is out of sync, but we can't quite put our finger on what it is. We just know that it's not the way we expected it to be—with ourselves, our families, or our other intimate relationships.

As you continue on in this book, perhaps with the goal of increasing the level of intimacy in your own family, you may be considering:

- how you could "start over again" and put your relationships on a more honest and open basis

- how you can overcome your reluctance, for fear

of being "inconsiderate" or "impolite," to say how you feel

• how to get closer to your children, or your parents, to connect with them

• how to achieve the deeper relationships that you constantly seek that never seem to pan out

• how to dispel the dread of family occasions that leave you feeling alone in the world despite having people around you.

Most of us have found ourselves in one of these situations at some point, and wanted more intimacy in our lives. Perhaps we feel a total lack of intimacy with our own biological families and don't know where else—or *how* else—to find it. Yet we want the closeness associated with that word, the unconditional love and support that "family" is supposed to provide.

This book offers some new ways of looking at intimacy and family, as well as some new ways of putting the two concepts together so that you can achieve your goals of closeness and support. We will explore:

• what intimacy is, and what it is not

• the specific beliefs, attitudes, habits, and myths that block our experience of intimacy

• how to create intimacy in our biological families

• how to create a new family when our biological family is no longer living or if intimacy with them seems impossible

What I hope to demonstrate in this book is that intimacy isn't something that happens to a person who is good enough, or lucky enough, or smart enough; it is something you can choose to have in your life or not, something that you can create at will, and something you can begin to achieve today even if you have never experienced it before. It is not restricted to or dependent upon the actions of other people. There is no "right" or "wrong" way to go about achieving it, no secret that some people can master and others cannot. The purpose of this book is to give you the keys to achieving intimacy in any relationship, and the special tools to create it within your own family—whether that family is related to you by blood or one you have chosen from among the people in your life.

We all have a natural impulse toward intimacy. We want union and closeness with other people. We want to love and be loved, to share our lives and hearts with others. We want to relax, open up, be ourselves, tell the truth, and have others love us *anyway*. And those things are available. Intimacy, after all, is the most natural thing in the world; it is also our highest calling as human beings, because in overcoming our barriers to intimacy we discover who we really are. We discover that we can live with ourselves; that we can accept ourselves, totally. And when we can accept ourselves, we find we can more easily accept others. Therefore, when relationships are truly intimate, they teach us to know and love ourselves as well as to know and love other people. These qualities bring forth the higher power within, and that is our highest expression and fulfillment. When we share it with our family—biological or "chosen"—the process becomes synergistic.

As we proceed to explore the ways in which we can create an intimate family, it is important to keep in mind that it is not always easy or comfortable, but it gives us the only things we really want in life—self-knowledge, love, and a connection with our higher power. These things are our birthright. We have only to reach out for them, look within ourselves for our deepest truth, share that truth with others, and they will be ours.

CHAPTER ONE

A FRESH START

Most of us have wished at some point that we could start all over in our relationships with family, friends, and lovers.

The good news is: You can!

The caution is: You will need to explore some new paths in order to arrive at a different destination, and traveling new roads can be challenging. In this chapter, we will look at some of the reasons why our past efforts to achieve intimacy in our relationships and family haven't worked, and set forth some new approaches that do.

Let's start with the story of Jane, a thirty-seven-year-old mother of two sons, ages eleven and fourteen, who came to me for counseling. Jane vaguely suspected something was wrong in her relationships, but her presenting symptom was exhaustion. "I can't put my finger on it," she said, "but everything seems wrong. This should be a wonderful time in my life. I have a good marriage and two great kids, but I feel like I'm just going through the motions."

When I asked Jane what was happening at home, she said she just felt deadened, as if her life consisted only of doing laundry, car-pooling to soccer games, fixing dinner, and entertaining her husband's business associates. She had considered going back to work, but she was sure her husband, Mike, a successful contractor, wouldn't appreciate the idea. Open-minded as he was, Mike didn't believe women should work outside the home when their children were still young. In fact, Jane didn't believe it, either. Although her mother had been an early feminist who founded a highly successful advertising agency, Jane had always resented her mother's activities and absences.

Jane thought that boredom might be her problem. But as we continued to talk, it became clear that Jane had very little interaction with her family beyond surface matters. She and Mike discussed his day at work, her day chauffeuring the kids. On occasion they gossiped about their friends, commenting on who got drunk at the office party, who had just lost a job or been hired away for an inordinate amount of money, and who was sleeping with whom. But they seldom discussed their relationship anymore, or even their personal dreams or goals. And they rarely fought or even disagreed. Nonetheless, Jane thought Mike treated her very nicely. He made sure she had everything she needed—or even wanted—at least materially.

"Mike is actually more attentive now than he used to be," Jane told me. "I really don't know what happened, but a year or so ago he told me to get household help, he bought me a fur coat, and he started coming home early from work. Even so, we don't seem to have much to say to each other except the ordinary litany of what happened during the day."

Aside from the occasional prank, the boys were not difficult children for Jane. Most of the time they were out of the house and involved in activities with school and friends. "I can't believe this is *our* family," she said. "I know we love each other, so why can't we talk? Why can't we share more of our dreams with each other? Why do we seem so distant?"

At some point, nearly every family finds itself in this kind of bind. The love is there, but somehow the connections just aren't being made. My own diagnosis of Jane's situation differed from her own. Jane's exhaustion wasn't from boredom: it was from loneliness and the strain of not being able to "get through" to the people closest to her. The communication system had broken down.

There are many reasons why this happens. One of them is simply the matter of time. Family members get busy with their various activities and aren't together long enough to get comfortable, much less intimate. In Jane's case, for example, the long walks she and Mike used to take had been preempted by the boys' evening soccer games, Mike's heavy work load, and Jane's volunteer activities with Suicide Prevention.

Another problem in some families these days is that members have such a variety of recreational choices. Equipped with a minimum of two cars, they can go in eight different directions and still be home for dinner—albeit a hasty one, since they now have to catch up on homework, laundry, and household repairs.

The situation Jane found herself in seemed to demonstrate how easy it is even for families who love one another to fall into nonintimate ways of behaving and relating.

What Intimacy is *Not*

There are many variations on the theme, but most of us grow up with a vague notion that intimacy is something warm, cozy, and comfortable. We have an unrealistic belief that in our intimate relationships we will be able to tell one another our secrets and express all our feelings without anyone getting hurt or angry. We're also inclined to think that once this mysterious "intimacy" is achieved, then everyone will be home free. Upsets or hurt feelings will disappear and everyone will feel close and secure. Needless to say, these ideas have little to do with true intimacy.

In my own practice I have observed that women are especially apt to equate intimacy with telling one another everything they are *feeling*. Many women are inclined to pump, prod, beg, wheedle, and criticize the man in their life who doesn't share every emotion that flashes through his head. Naturally, the men feel pushed up against the wall. They want nothing more than to retreat, which aggravates matters. Conversely, men often view intimacy as the ability just to sit quietly with someone and listen, without having to talk about how they feel. Sometimes a man may talk about what happened at work to a wife who is less interested in daily events and more interested in how he experienced them.

Many theories are expressed as to why men and women define intimacy as differently as they do. I believe men are taught to shut off feelings from the time they are very young. They're told to "act like a man" (which usually means "don't cry"), "keep a stiff upper lip," and "don't be a sissy." Girls, on the other hand, are given permission to express hurt and sorrow and are praised for being sensitive to the feelings of others.

Some theorists now believe that genetics plays more of a role in communication behaviors than was previously thought and that men and women are born with different tendencies. Regardless of the reasons, in my work I do see women begging for more communication about feelings and men begging their mates to understand that talking about work *is* talking about their feelings.

In fact, intimacy is not necessarily being achieved simply because feelings are discussed. And it *can* prevail when one is talking about work—or even football. I hope to show why this is so as we proceed.

Another area of confusion has to do with how others relate to us. Many people believe that intimacy cannot exist without our total acceptance of one another. The misconception exists that if people really love us, they will accept everything about us without question.

Many times one of my clients will complain, "My ———— just doesn't love me." (Fill in the blank with mother, spouse, father, etc. It doesn't matter because it's all the same.) As I pursue the issue and ask what they mean, they will say, "Well, he [or she] just doesn't accept me the way I am. He [or she] is always criticizing me."

In other words, he or she won't tolerate every little trait or unpleasant habit my client has. And that pattern of behavior, to many people, equals a denial of love.

The other side of this coin, of course, is the individual who wants to be able to accept everything about his or her intimates. The implied message here is that love equals total approval. Sometimes when we want to be intimate with another person, we ask him in one way or another to tell us who he really is. When he does, our internal response is often, "Oh, wait a minute. That's not what I mean at all. I wanted you to tell me who you really are, but I wanted that person to be someone I approved of and liked! Someone I found acceptable and who was okay with me. Not *that!*"

Mike learned early in his relationship with Jane that certain revelations were not appreciated, even when asked for. Jane always wanted to know which women Mike found attractive at parties or at the office. Invariably, Mike would admit that "the blonde with the blue eyes and long legs was pretty cute." Jane, with her brown hair, brown eyes, and short legs, would sulk for days after one of these episodes. First of all, it infuriated her that Mike found any other woman attractive. That by itself was objectionable. And that the women he liked to look at were Jane's exact opposite made Mike's response totally unacceptable. She thought he was utterly heartless for telling her the truth. And she took it personally.

The fact is, we don't always find everything about other people acceptable or likable. We're all human beings with certain prejudices and judgments, opinions and points of view, buttons or "hot spots" that make us angry, hurt, or defensive—at least at first.

Jane's "hot spots" reflected her own dissatisfaction with herself. As we talked, I learned that Jane had never liked her legs. In fact, she'd never liked her mother's short legs.

From the time she was old enough to notice, she preferred long legs. Her best friend's mother was a model whom Jane respected and admired. Jane wanted legs like that. Mike's reaction wasn't really the problem, except that it illuminated Jane's already formed prejudice. This is an important point: *Our unwillingness to face our own prejudices is often a major barrier to intimacy.*

Another common idea many of us have about our relationships is that the person with whom we are intimate will fulfill all our needs. No matter how hard Jane or Mike tried, they couldn't possibly be everything to each other. If Jane dislikes her own legs, all the praise in the world from Mike isn't going to change her self-image. Rather it will fall on deaf ears. And yet in my work I see case after case in which people are miserable because someone else isn't making them feel happy, excited, beautiful, worthwhile, interested, enthusiastic, loving, joyful, sensual, or whatever else they believe someone should be "giving" them in the relationship. Yet no one person can—no matter how much of a person he or she is.

In attempting to define intimacy it is also important to be clear that intimacy is not sex. This doesn't mean that sex is never intimate. It just means that sex isn't *automatically* intimate. Sex and intimacy are often confused with one another because sex intrinsically has some of the components of intimacy. Clearly, a great deal is revealed during sex: emotions, attitudes, physical appearance. Orgasm is frequently experienced as loss of control, and momentary though it may be, that's enough to make most people feel exceedingly vulnerable. These feelings of vulnerability are equated with self-revelation, which in turn is erroneously equated with intimacy.

But assumptions about sex and intimacy can, and do, lead to devastating relationship problems. If, for me, sex equals intimacy, while for you, it's just good exercise, then we may get into deep trouble as we form our ties.

Similarly, if I believe that intimacy can take place only within a sexual relationship, then my opportunities for in-

timacy and its benefits are severely limited unless I intend to
have a number of sexual partners of both sexes.

Of course, a sexual relationship can be exceedingly intimate. When it is, sex becomes love—the making of which
is an unsurpassed opportunity for full self-expression for you
and the one you love.

So intimacy is not a matter of having your needs fulfilled.
It is not the act of being completely accepted or accepting,
not revealing your deepest feelings, not being warm and cozy,
or not having sex, although each of those things may occur
in an intimate relationship.

Returning once again to Jane, she had several of these
misconceptions about intimacy. She had expectations that
could never be met, because the people in her family were
all human. Before she could start dealing with her problems,
she needed to gain a better understanding of what intimacy
is and how it is achieved.

What Intimacy Is

The Latin roots of "intimacy" are *intimare*, which means "to
announce" or "to make known," and *intimus*, which means
"innermost." True intimacy is *making your innermost self known
to others and allowing them to make themselves known to you*. It
sounds simple, but as you might expect, it can be difficult to
achieve. After all, if we have spent twenty, thirty, forty, or
more years communicating in a basically nonintimate way,
it's going to take some commitment and practice to change
that.

It's hard for most of us to imagine what it would be like
to let people know your thoughts and feelings without having
to edit or second-guess yourself—and to allow others the
same privilege. Jane's reaction to the idea was, "That would
be fantastic, but it might not be worth it. I can imagine the
fights we'd get into."

But there's nothing to fight about when you're simply

revealing yourself. What causes problems is that many of us use intimacy as an excuse to convey to others our opinions, judgments, and beliefs about *them*. It is often the case that when we start telling the truth, the first comments out of our mouths are negative thoughts and feelings about our companion, which in turn trigger negative thoughts and feelings in them. When we first try revealing our innermost selves, many people spew forth an uncontrollable dump of negative remarks that *do* provoke a fight. This fact makes many of us afraid to be "intimate." We equate it with Mother's tirades, Father's rages, and our own temper tantrums or outbursts.

What we don't realize is that conscious, direct, and immediate communication precludes the stockpiling of ammunition and makes intimacy quite manageable. Immediate communication does not mean revealing every thought or feeling that crosses our mind. It does mean creating opportunities for timely and *appropriate* communication.

Nor does making ourselves known to others and allowing them to make themselves known to us mean making known just the "good" parts. Most of us are quite willing to reveal the kind, helpful, wonderful parts of ourselves, but we aren't so eager for other people to find out about the "bad" parts, the jealousies, resentments, anger, and pettiness we fear spoils the picture of an "acceptable" person. When we must portray ourselves as "acceptable," the reality often is that we don't find ourselves acceptable at all. This makes us exceedingly vulnerable to the whims of others.

Let's examine Jane for a moment. Her inability, or unwillingness, to accept her short legs makes her completely vulnerable to Mike's comments about other women. If she addresses the subject, Mike might accuse her of being jealous, possessive, unreasonable, suffering from low self-esteem, and petty—an entire litany of human failings. Even if she doesn't impart her true feelings to Mike, she's apt to think these things about herself. In order to fend off the feelings, she may become defensive or self-righteous, and blame Mike for how she feels. But Jane intensely dislikes defensive, self-

righteous, blaming people. So either way she turns, she's
trapped by her own humanness—unless she begins to learn
to accept it.

Jane can spend all day saying Mike "shouldn't" like long
legs and blond hair, or he "should" phrase his comments in
an acceptable way. But these avenues simply won't work because (1) Jane can't change Mike or the way he feels, (2) Mike
can't help it if he likes blondes and long legs, and (3) the real
problem is in Jane's lack of self-acceptance.

In addition to seeing only the good in ourselves, we
would often rather see only the "good" parts of those we are
close to, rather than be exposed to their more human qualities
(unless we want them to look "bad" so we can look "good").

The kind of intimacy we are exploring in this book is
designed to bring an end to all that, or at least an awareness
of it and a willingness to move beyond it. Intimacy means
allowing ourselves and others to be "who we are not" as well
as "who we are." In Jane's case, she had let Mike and the
boys know only "who she was not." For example, Jane had
decided long ago that she was *not* like her mother. She was
not ambitious. Her primary interest was her family and she
would devote her time to taking care of them in a way that
she had not been taken care of. That's the kind of woman
Mike had married, and that's how she intended to be. As far
as Jane was concerned, feminism was for the birds.

But as we talked, Jane began to see that she had other
dimensions, and they seemed threatening. She feared that
revealing them could really shake up her marriage. The fact
was, she did have some ambitions that she wanted to fulfill.
The problem was not that she was bored by her somewhat
mundane life, but that she feared the results of sharing these
dimensions first with herself, and then with her family.

She was afraid of being thought selfish and unapprecia-
tive. She was afraid of the resentment that had built up within
herself over the years. She was afraid of becoming unavailable to her family. And she was panicked at the thought of
their reactions to the truth. Surely they would feel toward

her the way she felt toward her own mother—abandoned, neglected, and bitter. Initially, the idea of confronting all these reactions was out of the question, but as Jane was to discover, often we have to go through a period of negative expression before we can get to the positive emotions. If there is no room for the more "human" parts of us, we never get beyond them to the love.

Most people find that intimacy is well worth the discomfort, however, because it opens up a whole new way of relating—to themselves and to other people.

When you begin to express yourself and reveal your own truth, the first things you discover may not be your deepest truth. But you will never get to your deepest truth unless you give yourself permission to express what covers it. The part of the dynamics of intimacy that is often ignored is that this freedom of revelation is a two-way street. As you reveal yourself to others, you must become willing to allow them to reveal themselves to you.

Too often my clients think that self-expression means blurting what they think and feel to someone else without any consequence. Or they use the fear of repercussion as an excuse for remaining silent.

Often a client will ask something like, "Why did he get so upset? I just told him I was sick of faking orgasms all these years, and I wasn't going to do it anymore. I was just telling him the truth." We need to understand that people will react to such revelations. And the reactions are justified. Yet some of my clients use the anticipated reaction as an excuse for not divulging anything. They'll say, "Well, I'd like to tell him I've been faking orgasms for twenty years, but his ego just wouldn't tolerate it. I think he'd go off the bridge." Suffice it to say that neither attitude promotes intimacy.

Jane began to see how all of this worked in her relationship with Mike and her sons. Having made herself aware of some issues, Jane now needed to be willing to reveal them. She *did* have personal ambitions. She didn't want to devote

her entire life, every minute, to her family any longer. At
the same time, she did love her husband and children and
wanted to be available to them. In the process of communicating these things, Jane had to confess that at times she
felt like blaming them for her unhappiness. She told Mike
she appreciated fur coats and household help, but that she
wished they could talk about something more meaningful
than his latest client or her bridge game. She mentioned that
she might want to go back to work and that she resented his
ideas about working women, even though she held some of
those ideas herself.

She knew, in saying these things, that she might be upsetting the applecart, and she was right.

Mike's initial reaction was one of fear. He didn't want a
working wife. He wanted a mother for his children who
stayed home, just as his mother had. His response to Jane
was hostile.

"So you want to be like your mother? Never around,
talking only about her latest big deal? Your mother is the
most selfish woman in the world! Doesn't even have time to
visit her grandchildren! Divorced twice. Is that what *you*
want?"

Jane was seeing a part of Mike she'd never seen before.
He seemed downright vicious now, reacting as though he
knew where her soft spot was and going straight for it. Jane's
initial reaction was to retreat, but she could see what was
happening. First, she had revealed some uncomfortable
truths to herself. Next, she allowed herself to express them
to Mike and gave him a chance to express himself to her.
She could now see why she had never revealed herself before.
She was afraid of this juncture, and she was afraid of getting
stuck there.

But she didn't.

The next step for Jane was to discover and reveal her
deeper truths and to give Mike the opportunity to do the
same. So she continued on and told Mike that she loved him

and the boys, that she had no intention of leaving him, and that if she did take a job her family would still come first. Rather than becoming defensive about her mother, she told Mike that she had some fear of being like her and asked for feedback and support so as not to become unavailable to her family.

She then asked Mike to be frank with her, to tell her if she seemed distant and preoccupied, or appeared to be ignoring him or the children.

At first Mike wasn't too interested. He became sullen and uncommunicative. But as Jane let go of her past resentment and took more responsibility for her own happiness, and as she became more and more willing to communicate despite her fears of repercussion, Mike became less afraid of his own reactions. He began to realize that Jane really did love him and he became less threatened at the idea of her going out into the world. He finally became willing to confess a few scary truths to himself, one of which was that he believed working women were easy prey to other men.

This idea was based on personal experience: He had had a brief affair with the wife of one of his competitors. Following the affair, Mike had felt so guilty he showered Jane with gifts, including a fur coat and a maid, and tried in his own way to make it up by coming home early and being around the house more. But until he began to respond intimately these things didn't make the situation better.

By the time Jane discovered the affair through a "good friend," it was long over. At first she was furious and accused him of being a hypocritical chauvinist. She was hurt and bewildered because she had been trying so hard to be the perfect wife. How could he accuse her of threatening the family after doing something like this?

Fortunately, Mike was able to respond. "I never wanted to hurt you. I can't explain it or excuse it. I just want you to know how much I love you and how bad I feel about what I did. I can understand now why I'm so afraid to have you out working where there are guys like me around!"

Jane couldn't suppress a smile. Mike had never been so honest before. For the first time, she could truly see who Mike was and who he was not.

She and Mike continued to work things out, and the boys, with only an occasional complaint, adjusted nicely after Jane took a part-time job in her mother's advertising agency.

In intimate relationships, we learn that, although we may not be the people we *wish* we were, we are also not the people we're *afraid* we are. We learn, too, what our intimates wish and fear about themselves. In the process of making ourselves known, we begin to deal with wishes and fears for what they are, rather than as reality. Intimacy takes courage because, as you can see with Jane and Mike, each new revelation causes a shift in the relationship. Such movement is scary. It momentarily destabilizes the relationship and there's no way to know how, or if, things will resettle, but the alternative is impotence caused by the repetition of old patterns and ultimately the kind of deadness that Jane had begun to feel.

Whom Do You Trust?

Many who have ventured into the same arena as Jane have discovered that there is vulnerability in intimacy, because the other person in the relationship comes to know your weak spots. You can't open yourself up to others and then say, "But don't hurt me with the information you have about me now." They may hurt you, whether or not they intend to. There is only one person you have to trust in order to be intimate with another: yourself. You have to trust that you will be able to handle matters even if your partner seems to use the information against you.

In the situation between Jane and Mike, there was lots of room for each to feel vulnerable. Mike knew Jane was afraid of being like her mother. In an argument he could easily attack her with that information. Jane could dredge up Mike's affair anytime she wanted to. So they each must be able to trust their own reactions to an attack.

They must know that they can withstand hearing things about themselves that they would prefer to avoid, without letting the information devastate them. Only when they trust their ability to face themselves can they begin to trust each other. Otherwise, they are doomed to spend a good part of their lives defending themselves against self-discovery.

This trust arises when each is genuinely willing to be human, to have faults, to be imperfect. If I'm not afraid of my imperfections, you can't use them as a weapon against me. My natural reaction, when attacked or accused, is to defend. But if I can accept that not everyone sees me as perfect, I have nothing to defend against.

Coupled with the willingness to be human is the ability to forgive yourself and others for not being "perfect" according to your ideals. The faster Jane forgives her mother for not living up to Jane's expectations, the faster she can forgive herself and the less vulnerable she will be to Mike's attacks. The faster Mike forgives himself for making a mistake according to his own standards, the less vulnerable he will be to Jane's accusations. But forgiveness does not mean living without pain or sorrow. Mike and Jane can feel the sorrow for their actions (which is all that "I'm sorry" means) without feeling "to blame" for being human.

The problem with blaming is that it resolves nothing. It serves only to tear apart. In fact, the word "blame" comes from "blaspheme," which means "to desecrate." The moment we blame, we desecrate (or de-sacred) the one we are blaming, be it ourselves or someone else. Intimacy cannot exist in a blaming atmosphere. Intimacy must be nurtured in an atmosphere of wholeness, or as the sages might say, holiness.

Why We Crave Intimacy

With all this risk and discomfort, why does intimacy remain such a basic human desire? I believe it is because intimacy gives us the experience of union, of being one with other people. When we know that we are one with others, love is all that exists. And love is the most basic human desire.

Intimacy is not something you do; it is a way of being. It is a natural state, in that knowing and loving ourselves and others is a natural state.

On some level, we know that we are all one—but we have forgotten. Intimacy is the means to remembering and expressing our union. We experience this union through the part of us that is the God within, the Higher Power, or whatever words you use to describe our connection with the infinite. The more we improve our connection with our inner soul or spirit, the more it is reflected in our relationships with others.

Mike began to experience his connection with his inner strength as he let go of his old ideas about how Jane "should be." When he realized Jane was not going to return to her previous status as the family's servant and caretaker, Mike saw that he had to make some choices. He could be miserable and blame Jane for it. He could divorce her and find someone else to wait on him. Or he could realize that loving her meant letting her develop herself fully, which would place him in a position of developing himself more fully.

As he let go of needing Jane in the old ways, he began to discover parts of himself that he really liked. He saw that he could be generous, supportive, forgiving, patient—and he could even do the laundry without the white clothes turning blue. Surprisingly, to Mike, the more he began to respect himself, the more he respected Jane. And the more he loved himself, the more he loved Jane. For the first time, he began to have a glimmer of something greater than his own ego; something he now chooses to call God. It is the "something" which enables him to get outside of himself long enough to forget his fears of self-disclosure and which therefore gives him the power to experience intimacy.

Until we develop this connection with our higher power, we must adopt barriers to experiencing intimacy and love—defenses, decisions, judgments, prejudices, reactions, beliefs, and opinions about how things are—to protect ourselves from being hurt. Ironically, they are the very things that hurt us because they keep us from loving. The way out, the way beyond these barriers, is to become aware of them. Once we begin to make ourselves known and allow others to do the same in our presence, it quickly becomes clear just where those barriers are.

Then we can deal with them. We can choose to cling to our beliefs and reactions, or we can simply let go of them so we can love.

Finally, intimacy requires friendship. A friend is an ally, a supporter. Allies are joined or united for a specific purpose. The purpose of friendship is support. Don't even pretend to be intimate with someone you cannot support. And don't expect them to be intimate with you. Unless I know you support me, I cannot, and should not, trust myself with you. But it's important to remember that support may not always look the way I expect it to. My friends are my allies in my becoming, in the words of the U.S. Army, "all that I can be."

Friendship, then, is the human foundation of intimacy. Without it, true intimacy cannot take place.

Robot and Spirit

There is a singular aspect of human nature that makes intimacy the adventure it is. It also can make the achievement of intimacy a difficult task. I call it the Robot. The Robot is our "reactive" self—that part of us that operates automatically, without our consent or approval.

It's as though we are a computer full of programs just

waiting to be activated. On our chest is the keyboard. Someone punches the key, and off we go. Sometimes we have no
more control over what our reaction is going to be than any
computer has when the operator pushes the button. The
thing we do have control over is whether or not we *act* on
our reaction. But even that control exists only when we understand what is going on. If we think our reactions are real,
we are going to act on them as though they are real. In other
words, it doesn't matter if I really see a bear or merely *think*
I see a bear. My *reaction* will be the same. My blood will race,
my heart will pound, my body will tighten, saliva increase. I
will think "danger" and "protection"; my emotions will include fear and maybe anger for being in this predicament.
I will feel impelled to act in order to save myself. None of
this is in my control. The only thing in my control at this
point is whether to run, freeze, walk up to the bear and say
"hi," stand there long enough to see if it really *is* a bear, laugh
at myself for thinking that a stuffed bear was real, and so on.

So my automatic reactions are not in my control. My
actions are. But, and I repeat myself here because this is such
an important point, even my actions are not in my control
as long as I believe I am the Robot. The Robot is our survival
mechanism. Without it we might put our hand on a burning
stove, walk in front of trucks, and forget not to breathe under
water. Our inclination is to identify with that which can save
us, and so we identify strongly with the Robot, sometimes to
the point of relinquishing our ability to choose. The Robot
then becomes both the program *and* the programmer. It
becomes entirely self-serving and will destroy us in order to
preserve itself and its program.

This is the process that occurs during addiction and is
why it is so difficult to reason with an active addict. The
program says, "This substance equals survival." And the addict will use until he can separate himself from the program
and say to his Robot, "Well, I know you think that's true, but
I'm willing to take the risk that it's not true. I'm willing to

give up the substance even if you *are* right." Until that time, the addict is doomed. Not by the addiction, but by the belief that he and the Robot are one.

Now think about a time when you reacted to a situation in a way that you knew ahead of time could only make things worse. You blurted out a remark, drank too much alcohol, swore at someone. Chances are you were feeling angry and fearful when you did it and were sorry afterward. But you felt that you couldn't help it at the time. That's the Robot in operation. It has made decisions and judgments in the past —usually very early in life—against which it measures current experience. And if the past experiences were painful, the Robot will use all of its wiles to avoid those experiences now. For the Robot, there is no present. All interpretation is based on the past and the fear of a painful experience.

In fact, the Robot creates a sort of mental file cabinet of decisions based on previous experiences. The purpose of the file cabinet is to rule out any experience that, based on precedent, could be expected to cause pain or threaten survival. When it sees a "bad" experience coming, the Robot will do anything in order to block that experience. It is the Robot's defensive action that can make us flee from another person, rationalize that the other person is somehow "wrong," become *oblivious*—*anything* to avoid freely relating to the person and risking being hurt.

Once established, the contents of this file cabinet become exceedingly durable and difficult to change. It's as if giving up the file cabinet would be tantamount to giving up all our protection and armor.

So the Robot must defend itself (and its decisions) at all costs. It must always be "right" about what it has decided.

In my experience I have seen people and relationships die of "rightness." The fellow who knew he had the right-of-way at the intersection may have been "right," but he isn't around to talk about it, since he was clobbered by the other car.

Many people have been "right" about something their

spouse did "wrong," but they aren't in the relationship any longer. The spouse got sick of being the scapegoat and got a divorce.

Sadly, Robots can become more and more "right" as well as more fixed and rigid over time. Once the robot has come to a conclusion—for example, "people you love will abandon you"—it collects information that confirms this belief and creates an aggregate of similar experiences to justify the initial decision.

Molly, a friend of Jane's, had what I call an "abandonment button." She had never felt loved by her father, a workaholic M.D. who had little time for the family. Her mother and sister died from a freak paint-inhalation accident when Molly was ten, and Molly's Robot decided that anyone she loved would leave her, or at least be unavailable to her.

Not at all surprisingly, Molly was forever getting tangled up in relationships with married men who would eventually go back to their wives, or be unavailable on holidays, or not let her call the office. Finally, she ran into Tom, her high school sweetheart, who had carried a torch for Molly for ten years and had never married. Tom doted on Molly. He was always available. He called her day and night. And what was Molly's reaction? For about two weeks she was in heaven. And then she began to believe that Tom was a wimp. He just didn't have any backbone. He was always hanging around and she was getting bored with him. One day she announced she wasn't going to continue seeing him. Tom, of course, was devastated and felt totally abandoned. Within a month, Molly was dating Joe, her married supervisor at work, and her Robot's decision that "people you love will abandon you" remained intact, not only for her but for Tom now also.

This kind of thinking and behavior, which all human beings have in one degree or another, wreaks havoc with our desire and need for intimacy.

Fortunately, there is an antidote, an alternative, another aspect of each person that can help us see through the Robot's defenses. I call this part the Spirit.

Spirit is that part of us that is connected to our higher power—in fact, it *is* our higher power. It is the part of us that loves unconditionally, that doesn't feel the need to protect or defend, that is unafraid of telling the truth, opening ourselves to others and even being hurt. It is the part of us that loves, and knows we are one with everyone else, that inspires intimacy and is able to create it.

Spirit isn't afraid of experiencing all there is to experience in life and in ourselves. It isn't even afraid of the Robot. When we operate from Spirit, we aren't afraid of revealing ourselves to others, nor are we threatened by what others reveal about themselves to us. Spirit is the source of, and the reason for, true intimacy.

Connection with the higher power or Spirit isn't necessarily something religious or involved with traditional notions of God. It is an inner experience of peace and harmony with yourself and with your world. Not your Robot self, but your true self, which *is* Spirit. We can find that peace through intimacy in our relationships with others, but it's not something that others can give us. Each one of us has to discover it for ourselves. It is also an experience of self-sufficiency. I don't mean the "I can take care of myself, thank you" kind of self-sufficiency. A lot of those people are miserable. The connection with our higher power gives a deep inner feeling of self-worth, the ability to take care of our own feelings and our own needs.

Conscious Choice

We often have to make a conscious choice to operate from Spirit, because our first reaction is usually to operate from the Robot. The Robot is part of us, and it always will be. Remember, it is our survival mechanism. And it is a necessary part. The trick is not to get rid of the Robot, but to recognize it when it tries to take over and to move beyond it into Spirit.

Then Spirit becomes the operator and can direct the Robot into appropriate behavior.

I have one client who finds it very difficult to say the words "I love you," because when he was small, his mother told him she loved him and then turned around and wouldn't let him do things he wanted to do. No matter that the things he wanted to do—play in the street, stay up until midnight, and quit school—could have harmed him. His Robot decided that the words "I love you" were meaningless, so he has trouble saying them. Mothers often treat their children in this manner and most youngsters don't take it very seriously, but to this child it was an indication that he wasn't loved.

This example points up one other aspect of Robots. They are very individual. What one considers important, another considers petty. A person who has been beaten by his mother would think my client is making a ridiculous complaint. In attempting to create a context of intimacy, it's a good idea to remember that what was threatening to you may not have been threatening to someone else. Comparisons are dangerous.

There was a time when my own Robot couldn't tolerate anything it perceived as criticism. At some point when I was very young, my Robot decided that if people criticize you, then they don't love you. After I got married, this decision caused a lot of problems in my relationship with my husband. I couldn't stand to hear any of the things that bothered him in our relationship. Because he couldn't tell me the truth, there was no room for him to communicate *anything* to me, including the fact that he loved me. When there is no room to talk about the things we *don't* like, there is no room to feel or talk about the things we *do* like. We get deadlocked because of whatever it is we can't say.

It's hard to let go of being "right." I had looked very "right" in my relationship with my husband, because I appeared to be so open, warm, and communicative. After all, I talked to him about *my* feelings, about my mother, my friends, my work. But I couldn't stand to hear anything negative about myself or to say anything negative about him. The day came, however, when I realized my marriage was in real jeopardy. We had become excruciatingly polite and our marriage had become commensurately dead. The first thing I had to do was to recognize and reveal to myself and my husband the fact that my fear of criticism was stifling our relationship—which was no fun at all because it didn't make me look very good—and then I had to let go of it.

"Looking good" is a preoccupation of the Robot. Since the Robot is concerned with survival and being right in order to survive, looking bad could be dangerous. The Robot causes us to erect a facade consisting of qualities that are the opposite of what we're trying to disguise. If my fears are selfishness, greed, and anger, then you can bet my facade will include altruism, generosity, and sweetness.

One of my clients, Jim, has spent his life trying not to be like his violent, alcoholic father. Jim presented an image of iron self-control, gentle behavior, and kindness. The suppressed fears burst forth one day when Jim's wife teased him once too often about his incompetence as a handyman. Jim put his fist through the door in a rage that terrified both his wife and himself. The incident brought them to my office, where they subsequently learned new and more effective communication skills.

In an intimate relationship, there has to be room for facade and fears as well as for Spirit. We have to be able to bring them out and let them show in order to realize that we are neither who we *wish* we were nor who we're *afraid* we are, but that our true self is Spirit.

In order to let our fears surface, we must remember that the Robot blocks hurtful experiences. In fact, the Robot will block ecstatic experiences also, since they could be followed by a devastating crash. The Robot really doesn't want to experience much of anything. It prefers to compare, analyze, judge, reason, and figure things out based on its file cabinet of information. Experiencing has to do with the moment, now, without the encumbrances of the past or even the future. To the Robot, this is a terrifying concept, because how can it relate to something it doesn't understand?

None of this means that the Robot doesn't "feel" things. People are apt to believe that the Robot operates only at the level of the mind, the intellect. Actually, feelings are often as Robotic as rationalization. Notice how often people use their feelings as an excuse for what they do. "I don't *feel* like" or "I do *feel* like it," "My *feelings* are telling me": All are considered legitimate explanations for every kind of behavior. Many people set up their lives to ensure that they're whipped around by drama and therefore have an excuse for emotions over which they take no responsibility.

In this Robotic environment, intimacy is blocked, because intimacy occurs when one is truly open to all kinds of experiences—exhilarating, hurtful, uplifting, embarrassing, sad, happy. But in the end, the Robot is fighting a losing battle. Healthy growth is always toward Spirit, and Spirit is willing to experience anything.

When the Robot blocks certain experiences, those experiences keep presenting themselves over and over again. It's as though we are meant to have them, and we *will* have them—sooner or later. All the Robot's resistance does is make the process slower and more painful. *What we resist will persist*, because we need all our life experiences to complete ourselves, to know ourselves and all it means to be human.

In looking at our original example of Jane and Mike, we know that if Jane hadn't had the courage to talk with Mike, the marriage inevitably would have worsened until it reached a crisis that *forced* Jane to deal with it. It's even a good bet that, had she let her relationship with Mike deteriorate to the point where they separated, the next relationship she had would have presented her with a very similar situation.

Risk and Support

In the face of a risky or frightening experience—the kind the Robot tries to block—we need support, and the higher up the line that support comes from, the better. Being aware of the Spirit within us can be our best ally when dealing with the Robot's attempts at defense.

Let me recount the story of Alice, who came to me because, for the first time in her life, she had everything she wanted. Her marriage, her job, her home—even her horse —were exactly what she desired. Yet she wasn't able to experience the joy of having all those things. She finally became aware of a decision her Robot had made when she was six years old and her mother died: *If you have something you want, you will lose it and that will be devastating.*

For many years, this decision had prevented her from having the things she wanted, because the thought of losing them was so painful. Now she had them, but she was subtly trying to destroy them. She was withdrawing from her husband and finding fault with him because somehow, if he weren't so perfect, it wouldn't be so hard to lose him. Of course, in the process, she was losing him.

Fortunately, she realized what she was doing. She realized that her Robot was panicking at the thought of being out of control. She had to take her Robot firmly by the hand and say, "Okay, I see that you're afraid, but we're going to go through this anyway. We're not going to throw away all this just so that you don't have to be afraid. We're going to have it, and we're going to live with the fear of losing it, but we're also going to enjoy it."

That took a leap of faith—faith that the unknown benefits would outweigh the known fear. We're so in the habit of letting our Robot run the show that to act from Spirit and open ourselves up to new experience can be frightening. The one reason to make that leap of faith is that it makes us feel alive. It lets us go beyond the fear and gives us ourselves.

Life continuously gives us the opportunity to find out who we really are. We can never rid ourselves completely of the Robot, but we can choose whether to give power to it or to Spirit. The more we act from Spirit, the more we can realize that Spirit is not my Spirit or your Spirit, but *the* Spirit. It is the means by which the higher power expresses itself through each one of us. It is our means to the infinite, to every human possibility, to union and to love.

When I experience the Spirit in myself, it's easier to experience it in other people. I can see everybody in my life as just another manifestation of the Spirit within, even when they are acting from *their* Robots. They may have given over their power to the Robot temporarily, but the Spirit is there. At any moment, that Spirit can burst forth and manifest itself in some wonderful way, and it is more likely to do so if I make room for it by expressing the Spirit within me.

The Robot is terrified of losing its individuality. But in fact, it is only by taking the power from the Robot and giving it to the Spirit that our true individuality, identity, can come forth. The Spirit is our true nature. It will always find a means of expression, and each one of us plays out different aspects of its light.

Its ultimate purpose is to shine forth that light, and to love other expressions of itself. That is what happens in intimacy.

The Intimate Family

The highest purpose for a family is to provide an environment of support and love, a safe place from which we can go out into the world and express whatever the Spirit has chosen to manifest through us. It doesn't matter if we manifest the Spirit's light by being a dancer, a computer programmer, a blacksmith, an artist, a mother, or a farmer.

If the family supports us in that manifestation, then it supports the community and all of humankind.

In other words, as the family supports each of us in our individual pursuits and in the development of our special gifts, we can then make our contribution, through those gifts, to the world at large. Without the support of family, I would find it exceedingly difficult to write books, my daughters could have been blocked from pursuing their careers, and my husband might have had no one to turn to during a major career transition. I'm sure we would have survived. Perhaps we would have accomplished the same things. But having a supportive family surely has made it, if not easier, at least more bearable and at many times a lot of fun.

I believe we each want to make an individual contribution in our lifetime. When our ability to make that contribution is thwarted, we sometimes go into a decline and can even die. I've heard it said that only those of us who serve will have true satisfaction in life, and in my experience that's true.

As long as my life was basically about myself—my wants, my needs, my problems—it seemed empty and unfulfilling. But once I made a commitment to share my experience, strength, and hope with others, life became satisfying, interesting, and fun. Intimacy with my family and friends provides me with the nourishment for making my contribution—it nourishes the Spirit.

It is in the family—whether biological or "chosen"—that we are most likely to experience the Spirit, because it is here that intimacy is best fostered. We have the power to create intimacy, and to create family. At any moment, we can make a fresh start in our relationships with other people, just by choosing to do that.

Through this kind of intimacy, we become known to ourselves as well as to other people, and experience the joy of letting others become known to us. That is why we are here, and it is the only thing that will really make us happy.

QUESTIONS TO ASK YOURSELF

How do I define intimacy?
How do I picture my family in my mind?
What are my greatest flaws?
What do I do to cover them up?
What parts of me am I most afraid of?
Who in my family do I not want to be like?
What experiences do I hope to avoid in relationships?
What contributions do I want to make in my lifetime?

THINGS TO DO

Share these questions and your answers with someone.

CHAPTER TWO

THE CHANGING FAMILY

We don't need the Census Bureau to tell us that the American family is changing. More people than ever before in our history are getting divorced, and step families are common. More people live great distances from the places they were raised and have minimal contact with their biological families. More people choose to remain single, and more of those people adopt or have children of their own. In many families, both parents work outside the home. Grandparents are forming their own communities (where small children are permitted only at certain limited times), or spending their retirement traveling around the country in airstream trailers instead of baby-sitting. Very little is the way we expected it would be when we were growing up.

I believe that many of these changes are healthy. Any institution that supports individuals in their development must be able to change and grow itself. The shifts we are seeing in the family are a natural response to our own changing evolutionary needs.

The old pictures of families huddled around the fire,

picnicking on the town green every Sunday, and doing all the things that families were supposed to do often reflected no more true intimacy than we have now. There was a certain sense of belonging and togetherness, but there was also complacency and rigidity. Everyone knew the accepted, proper ways to speak and act, but there was very little opportunity for self-discovery or true intimacy.

Historically speaking, the "perfect family" we meet on television existed for only about forty years, if it existed at all. Prior to the turn of the century, whole families seldom survived the span of years we now think of as normal. Women died in childbirth with great frequency and men married two or three times in a lifetime. If the woman survived, often she was widowed by the time she was forty. And she was also considered middle-aged if not downright old by that time. It was rare for any couple to spend more than twenty years together, since one or both of them usually died before they reached the point where, today, they might divorce. Few families saw all of their children grow to adulthood. There was a much smaller middle class than exists today, and the majority of Americans lived with little security. Men and many women worked twelve hours a day, six days a week. There was no such thing as welfare or Social Security, and grown children were expected to care for their aging parents, who often lived with them.

Probably the type of family that existed longer than any other was the first human family, the tribe that banded together in order to survive when we were some of the smallest, weakest creatures on earth. We had only clubs and one another with which to defend against a hostile world. We needed each other badly. We had to have as many children as possible or we would become extinct. It was out of the question for the oldest son to go off somewhere and "find himself."

We still have those strong biological urges to create family. These instincts are what allowed us to survive as a species, and they remain a part of our physical and psychological makeup today.

The "perfect family" we see on television never even existed in most people's minds until World War II. Following the war, the middle class grew by leaps and bounds and it became a status symbol for the wife to stay home taking care of the children while the husband went out into the economic boom and made enough money to buy new homes, new cars, and college educations.

Even then, people often did not marry for intimacy. They married for emotional and economic security, for conformity, for partnership and companionship. It hasn't been until very recently, as women have been able to make their way in the work world on their own, and men have learned to cook and launder for themselves, that marriage for intimacy has become a real option.

Since the family began as a survival mechanism, we have always put a lot of energy into the idea of family. If your family didn't survive in those early days, then *you* probably wouldn't survive. That's no longer true, but often we act as if it were. Ideas of what the "perfect family" is are changing, but many myths remain and they are surrounded by the same kind of "charge" with which our ancestors held off the attacks of beasts.

Today we have many scenarios for the "perfect family," and most of us are hooked into at least one of them.

One person might say the "perfect family" lives on Elm Street in Middletown, U.S.A. Their house has a white picket fence, green shutters, and a beautiful lawn. Mommy and Daddy have a little boy, a little girl, a dog, and a parakeet, and everyone is happy and healthy. Mom bakes cookies, does volunteer work, and chauffeurs the kids around to their gymnastic and music lessons. Dad works hard to support the family, but also leads a Scout troop, helps with Little League, and belongs to the Rotary.

Then there is a more updated version of the "perfect

family." Maybe there's just one parent, the mother, but we remember from *Little Women* that it's okay to have a single parent as long as everyone deeply loves one another. The mother in this family has to work, of course, but she still comes home and cooks dinner and tucks everyone in. The kids do the dishes. The older daughter does the sewing; the son takes out the garbage and mows the lawn. There's a tragic element about the missing parent, but still, there's so much love!

Moving a little farther from Middletown, we have the picture of the city family with two working parents. He is a doctor and she is an attorney, just like the parents on *The Cosby Show*. Even though he works fifteen hours a day delivering babies and she tries cases before the Supreme Court, everybody has time to talk to each other. Upsets occur, but they all sit down immediately and work it out. People are patient with one another and know just what to say. The parents understand the kids, but they set reasonable limits on their behavior. The kids grow up without sexual stereotypes. The little girls play with trains and the little boys play with dolls. Everyone knows that they are loved, and that problems are all in good fun.

There may even be an orphan among the "perfect family" scenarios. She lives with her grandparents, like Heidi, but they keep up with the times and are not old fuddy-duddies. They love the little girl devotedly, buy her a computer, and with their support she goes to MIT and wins a Nobel Prize.

The thing all these "perfect families" have in common is *love*. Not just any old kind of love, but *perfect* love. In spite of everything, people communicate wonderfully. When they're impatient, tactless, or grouchy, it's just a setup for an easy, perfect resolution. When they do say unpleasant things, they are quick to apologize. They're all quite capable of reading one another's minds and figuring out just what the other person wants. They are sensitive, thoughtful, considerate mind readers, and love conquers all.

What is missing from all these versions of the "perfect family" is the recognition that change is hard, slow, and frustrating, with frequent backsliding. There isn't much room for human frailties in our ideas of the "perfect family."

Our myths of the "perfect family" present us with a no-win situation. On the one hand, family is an institution based on biological urges and physical survival. For many, it is still connected with emotional survival. No family wants to be ostracized from the community, and will band together to hide or change a member whose behavior might threaten its standing in the community. No one wants to be ostracized from his or her own family, and the thought of voluntarily separating from one's family is terrifying. No matter how enlightened or informed or modern we are, it *hurts* not to be connected with family.

But at the same time, we can never live up to the myth of the "perfect family," because we are human. In order to find happiness and intimacy in the family, we have to let go of these myths about what the family is. Most of them never had much basis in reality anyway, and even those myths that did were based on needs other than intimacy, needs that are now outmoded.

Intimacy as a primary goal for families is a new idea. We no longer need the protection of our family to survive mammoth attacks. We no longer need the family to survive economically. What we do need now is intimacy. That is the evolutionary frontier we are exploring.

What does "family" mean today? Dictionary definitions speak of "the basic biosocial unit" of "one or more adults living together and cooperating in the care and rearing of their own or adopted children," but there is also mention of "people bound together by philosophical, religious, or other convictions; a fellowship," and "individuals living under one roof or household."

The Latin root of "family" is *familia*, or "servant." To me, this suggests that the family's purpose is to serve both individuals and society. When individuals live within an intimate family, they are free to explore and develop them-selves. They can find and express their unique talents and make their own unique contributions both to the family and to society at large.

That is all any of us really want to do, and that is why I like to define family as "the people with whom you are in-timate." They may be your biological family, or they may not, but they will be the most important people in your life, be-cause, through your relationships with them, you will dis-cover yourself and your connection with your higher power.

The Family and Intimacy

Having a group of people with whom you can truly be your-self gives you the opportunity to develop and express your gifts and talents. It also brings the joy and fulfillment of watching those around you do the same. You have others around you to love, and to share not just the wonderful, exciting things in life, but the difficult or fearful times. It is a place to gather your strength, your forces, and your courage.

Intimacy is a human need. It is our nature to go beyond what we have done; our frontier now is not survival but wholeness, the discovery of our deepest selves and our con-nection with our higher power. That is a tall order, and we need support to do it. The family—whether biological or "chosen"—is where we find that support.

Family Roles

One thing that makes intimacy in the family so interesting and challenging is that, in every family, there are certain roles that have to be played out. Even these family roles have historical and biological roots.

In our ancestors' families, the father was usually the strongest physically, so it was his job to go out into the world and "hunt." Mother was the one who bore and nursed the children. The oldest child no doubt helped with the younger ones and became the model for his siblings. A prehistoric family would also have benefited by having a child who was fearless, who rebelled and kept things stirred up. The child who didn't seem to fit in anywhere and kept to himself might be the one to go off and start a new tribe. And every family needs a baby—a fun-loving, adorable, perhaps somewhat ir-responsible "mascot."

A number of psychologists, including Gail Smith and Sharon Wegsheider-Cruse, have identified contemporary equivalents of these roles: Father, Mother, Perfect Child (Hero), Rebel, Loner, and Charmer. Each will be assumed by someone, at some time, regardless of how many children there are in the family. The roles people play out will depend on the number and sex of the children, their order of birth, everyone's individual makeup, and many other variables. These roles are helpful, healthy, and even necessary. Family roles cause trouble only when they become rigid, when peo-ple begin to identify with their roles so strongly that they believe those roles are who they are.

In most families, people take turns playing various roles over the years. One child might start out as the Rebel, and in the course of growing up and even into adulthood, become the Perfect Child or even the Charmer. When one person changes roles, it upsets the balance and everyone else has to switch roles, too, in order to cover all the bases. If the Perfect Child suddenly decides he's going to be the Rebel, someone else has to fill that role of Perfect Child. Then whichever place *that* child left must be filled.

Generally speaking, the children's roles are determined by birth order, with the firstborn being the Perfect Child, the second being the Rebel, the third being the Loner, and the fourth being the Charmer. Since few families have four chil-

dren these days, one child may take on several of these iden-
tities. We will look more closely at this balancing act, or
homeostasis, after we have examined each role.

1. *Father.* Father is the breadwinner and represents the
family out in the world. He is fearless, protective, and the
"last word" on decisions relating to the physical survival of
the family. Father's role can force him into a position of
machismo which distances him from the family. Decisive, un-
flappable, father must always present a strong image. If he
and the family buy this propaganda, Dad has no room to
express his sensitive, gentle side. Who he really is is lost in
the shadow of his projected identity.

2. *Mother.* Mother is the nurturer or caretaker. She deals
with people's emotions, keeps the home fires burning, and
acts as the glue who keeps the family together. This role can
have some degree of guilt or victimhood attached to it.
Brought up to believe she exists for the sake of others, taught
that her primary concern must be for the feelings of others,
her identity is fed by acknowledgments of how thoughtful,
caring, and sensitive she is. To truly express herself might
jeopardize this carefully designed image and so she becomes
a victim of her family's whims. Should she occasionally break
character, the negative feedback is swift, the resulting guilt
overwhelming, and she is soon back to "normal."

Often when the mother has a career, someone else in
the family will take on the role of nurturer. Yet I am constantly amazed by the number of women who have children
later in life swearing that "I'm going to let my husband stay
home from work when the kids are sick" and "I'll be back to
work a month after the baby is born," but who prefer, once
they've actually had the baby, to stay home and take care of
it—testimony to an instinct that won't be denied.

Either role—that of career person or that of nurturer
—can be healthy. Or these roles can be used to cover up
feelings of inadequacy and fear, creating distance through

absence or overprotectiveness. The "perfect mother syndrome" is also a great barrier to intimacy. Children with "perfect mothers" often spend their lives trying to prove that mother wasn't perfect. That, in fact, she had made an enormous mistake in life—namely, *them!*

3. *The Perfect Child.* This is usually the oldest child. He often has the highest IQ, which may be because he spends a great deal of time with his parents when he is young and is exposed to their conversation and behavior. This child does well in school and then comes home and takes care of everyone else. He is very concerned about doing things the right way, achieving the most that he can, and behaving in a way that will please the big people with whom he lives.

He is often a perfectionist. He can't stand an uncapped tube of toothpaste, clothes lying around on the floor, an unbalanced checkbook. He takes on a lot, and does it all perfectly. He has a high need for control in his environment.

One of two things usually happens with the Perfect Child in his relationships:

(1) He gets approval for being good and achieving a lot, and then begins to think that the reason he is loved is that he *earned* it. He then draws the conclusion that he has to earn love by behaving well and trying hard. His identity becomes tied up with trying to please others. Or . . .

(2) If this child doesn't measure up to his parents' expectations—if he just doesn't have the right build to be a great athlete or the right brains to be a Nobel physicist—he may begin to *reject* authority and turn against the high standards that have been set for him. If this happens, he is likely to become not only rebellious but also very authoritarian himself. This puts him in a bind. He likes the power he feels when he bosses the younger kids around and tells them what to do. On the one hand, he resists authority, but he becomes the very thing he has rejected. It is hard for him to be intimate, because it's hard for him to reveal that he *is* the thing he most *hates*.

The Perfect Child often has very high self-esteem. This, too, can cause problems in obtaining intimacy. A person who has done so well and lived up to everybody's expectations so beautifully often has very little tolerance or understanding for those who haven't done the same thing.

The Perfect Child often avoids venturing out into situations or relationships where he might experience defeat. He doesn't want to put himself in positions where he might not succeed. This can be a barrier to intimacy as well, since intimate relationships are always risky.

The Perfect Child is apt to be smarter, more gifted, better behaved, and more responsible than his brothers and sisters. If he marries someone who is like one of his siblings—as many of us are inclined to do in our attempts to complete the Robot's unfinished business—then that person will never quite measure up, either.

It's often difficult to be in a relationship with a Perfect Child, because he has spent a lifetime insulating himself against criticism and anything that smacks of failure. Vulnerability is hard for him. He considers it rather stupid to put himself in vulnerable positions, and he doesn't do stupid things. Of course, he is not perfect; but he doesn't ever want to see that, and he doesn't want others to see it, either. His Robot believes that he has survived and earned approval by being perfect; to realize that he is *not* perfect would be a kind of death.

The Perfect Child often inspires admiration and respect, but he doesn't always inspire a lot of love. His Robot insists gruffly, "When you have admiration and respect, who needs love?" But somewhere deep within him, he hurts, because he doesn't feel lovable and works even harder so that he will at least have respect and admiration.

If you are in a relationship with one of these people, there is an almost irresistible temptation to poke holes in him or try to tear him down. Don't bother. It's an absolute waste of time. He won't even notice, or else he will argue circles around you. The only thing you can do in a relationship with a Perfect Child is to take care of yourself, not try to compete with him or outdo him, and simply be the most of who you are in the relationship. It's also important to have a sense of humor.

The Perfect Child may not criticize you with words; he doesn't have to. He just demonstrates every day how much better he is, and all your failings become more obvious in his presence. The best way to deal with this is to gain your own self-esteem by recognizing that you have chosen your own path, and chosen to flail around a bit in the process of self-discovery and risk-taking rather than doing everything perfectly all the time. All you can do is make yourself known to him, and let him take it or leave it. Rather than trying to measure up to his standards, you can just say, "This is how I am. I may mess up." If you can hold your own with a Perfect Child, you'll be in good shape to tackle intimacy with *anyone*.

4. *The Rebel.* If for some reason the firstborn has not become the Perfect Child—because he has followed the path of resisting authority or because some physical, mental, or emotional problem keeps him from playing that role—the second child will have to take on that position. Usually, however, the second child becomes the Rebel.

The second child arrives on the scene to find these three perfect people—two huge, all-powerful parents and a Perfect Child—existing in a sort of triumvirate. It is not an inviting prospect. How is he ever going to measure up, or even find a place in this family? He isn't big or powerful, and there is no way he can ever be as good as the Perfect Child, who by now has at least a year of life under his belt and probably more. So the second child decides he's going to do something else. His Robot wants attention at any cost, and the only way this child can hope to get attention is by doing just the *opposite* of what everyone else has done.

He will do "bad" things, be the maverick, stir things up a bit. No one else is doing that, so he is bound to get attention and become special in that way. He may act out in obvious ways like breaking windows, or he may do something more subtle, like getting C's instead of A's and B's like the Perfect Child. He often becomes the scapegoat, the catalyst for all the family's problems.

I was a second child, and I realized early on that there was simply no way I could compete with my older sister. She was very beautiful, a talented musician, and an excellent student who helped with the housework and then went off into a corner and read quietly. So the way I got attention was by being the one who *couldn't* read. Dyslexia prevented me from reading until I was in fourth grade, and I got just as much attention for not reading as my sister did for reading, so it worked out very well.

The Rebel may resist authority on all levels. He may be the liberal in the family. He will be intolerant in a different way from the Perfect Child; he will be intolerant of intolerance. He won't be able to stand people who put other people down. He will fight for the underdog, and he will often marry someone his parents wished he hadn't.

If you marry a Rebel, you may find that there is another side behind the liberal facade and the resistance to authority. He may have very strong opinions about things and be quite capable of putting others down, but the people he puts down will be people who act superior. The Rebel does not want to be reminded of feeling *inferior* or not as good as other people, particularly his Perfect Child sibling. He also won't want to find out that he is judgmental, because he puts people down for being judgmental.

5. *The Loner.* The third child coming on the scene may perceive, "One of these kids is perfect and the other is aggressively *not* perfect. Those two roles are filled. Nobody really needs me for anything." Initially, of course, this child will be the baby. Everyone will give him lots of attention for being little and cute and adorable, but when the *next* child comes along, then *that* child becomes the Charmer and the third child has nowhere to go.

This child may be somewhat withdrawn. He may be the reader, the painter, the one who goes off by himself and likes to be alone. He doesn't like all the hassle and confusion and noise. But he still has a Robot and, one way or another, he is going to get attention. If you walk into a room full of people who are talking and interacting, and then see one person standing off by himself looking uncomfortable, who is the person you really notice? Where is your attention focused? You may go about your business and not really interact with him, but you are always aware of his presence. You worry about him and wonder if he is okay. This is how the Loner gets attention.

The decision the Loner's Robot has made is that he survives by withdrawing, so an intimate relationship with him may be difficult. Naturally, the people he attracts are those who try to *keep* others from withdrawing. You may be tempted to go after him and cajole him into interacting. He wants you to do this, up to a point. He wants you to try, but he doesn't really want to come out of his shell. He has survived in the past by *not* coming out. He has been very quietly standing apart, judging everybody else and being secretly critical of them for interacting with one another. To enter into the fun would be a kind of capitulation.

It's hard to win in this situation. If you try to make him communicate, he doesn't like it. If you don't try to make him communicate, he doesn't like it. And he likes it least if you're a Perfect Child or a Rebel, because these are the last people he wants in his life.

6. *The Charmer.* By this time, the family dynamic is badly in need of someone who doesn't cause trouble, someone who is just a little darling.

The Charmer discovers very early that he has the power to get attention by making people feel good. All it takes is a smile from him, and Mom comes out of her funk. Dad may be grouchy with the other kids, but becomes suddenly jolly when the Charmer comes into the room. He learns that the

way to get along in the world is to be delightful and disarm-
ing. He also takes a look at everybody else and thinks, "I
want nothing to do with any of that. They're not very happy,
they don't brighten up anybody's life, they make *me* unhappy
. . . Who needs it?"

The difficulty with being in an intimate relationship with
a Charmer is that Charmers don't like to look bad. So if you
see through their facade, or act in ways that trigger their
"uncharming" characteristics, you will be blamed for their
lapse.

Charmers sometimes become Rebels as they move into
their teens, but they are usually able to charm their way out
of any real trouble. They are ones whom most of us wish our
son or daughter would date. They are popular and often
good-looking. They may be highly successful, but may also
suffer the "imposter syndrome" (not believing they really
deserve the good that comes their way) and can end up as
con artists. On some level, they may always believe they got
where they did because of their charm and not because of
their ability—and they may be right.

They don't mean to be manipulative, but you won't be
as likely to make demands on them as you would on other
people. And if they treat you badly, you'll be more likely to
overlook it.

Sometimes a parent will even take on one of the "children's roles," leaving, in effect, only one adult at the head
of the family. The roles people take on will always be *those
that get them the most attention.* We all want to be unique and
special, to be noticed, to make our individual contributions
and have them recognized.

This combination of roles seems to balance and stabilize
any group. They exist not only in each family but in all kinds
of groups and in society as a whole. We need to make room
for all of these roles, recognize their importance, and include
them in the functioning of the group. If one person isn't
allowed to play out his role, he will get more and more at-

tached to it, because on some level he knows it is important to the survival of the group. Because they now think they are the role, they can't make the shifts and changes necessary for a fluid, balanced dynamic.

Sometimes it looks as if certain roles don't contribute. We often want to make the Rebel or the Loner the scapegoat for any problems that come along, because we feel their behaviors are disruptive. We have to remember that *every* role is vital to the group, rather than feeling threatened because it looks as if one person is doing something different from the rest of us.

The key to all of this is *inclusion* rather than *exclusion*. When someone rebels or dissents in a group or family, it seems to wreak havoc on everybody else. Yet we need to have people who rebel and dissent. We know this as a nation; that is why we support free speech—because it encourages the exchange of new ideas. We also need to include the person who goes off by himself and thinks things through. It gives us a new and potentially valuable perspective. It's also nice to have someone around to entertain and charm us, to lighten things up and represent us in the world in a delightful way. And we need the perfectionist, the one who is concerned about detail and keeps things neat and clean, who reminds us to do things as well as we can.

Sometimes we have to look beneath the surface to see which roles people are actually playing. We think of the mother as the nurturer and caretaker, but that's not always the case, even if she stays home with her children all day. One mother might be a Perfect Child, a neatnik who drives everyone nuts because the house has to be kept in perfect order all the time. This leaves her little time for nurturing anyone. In fact, she may be a total nag. Another mother might be a Charmer who goes off and has lunch with her friends, takes the kids to the park, lets them finger-paint on the walls, and is delightful and creative, even if the house is in shambles. Someone on the outside might consider her to be a dreadful flake, but she may actually be far more nurturing than the drone who is home all day being the "perfect" wife and mother.

When people have permission to assume whatever role they need at the moment, then everyone can make themselves known, complete whatever they need to get from one role and move on to another. No one atrophies. Everyone has the freedom to acknowledge what role he is playing, to be responsible for it, and to recognize his contribution. The family is constantly moving and growing, providing an environment in which individuals can also move and grow.

An example of this kind of development took place in the Smith family, who originally came to see me about their teenage daughter's drinking.

Joan Smith and her husband, Hank, had strong ideas about family and parenting. They had both grown up in blue-collar families, but Joan had put Hank through law school and immediately retired from nursing as soon as he joined a law firm. She was not going to work outside the home and subject her children to the kind of childhood *she* had experienced with two working parents. Joan, the Perfect Child, did not want her own daughter to "have to" clean the house and take care of younger children, as Joan had done. Her children would have piano lessons, participate in extracurricular activities, be car-pooled, and go to the best schools in town. Hank's beliefs were equally strong. He would support her and never let her or their children experience the uncertainties he had grown up with because of his alcoholic father.

Into this "perfect" setting, Sarah was born. Bright, talented, and pretty, Sarah was all Hank and Joan could have hoped for. And then came Jill. From birth, Jill was hyperactive, colicky, and temperamental. Hank and Joan tried not to make comparisons—but it was difficult. Jill was so different from Sarah. And she really didn't measure up. She didn't even learn to read until she was nine.

Some other things were happening, too. Joan missed her career, but she couldn't admit it—not even to herself. The more unhappy she felt, the more energy she put into Sarah's talents, and the more Jill seemed to be the "cause" of her unhappiness.

By the time Tom came along, an unexpected child, the situation was pretty much of a mess.

Hank, working hard, bringing home money, providing a lovely home, lessons, fine schools, and household help, could never have accepted the fact that Joan was miserable because she missed working and having an identity of her own. Joan couldn't have accepted it, either. Sarah was still "perfect," Jill was always creating upsets, and it didn't take Tom long to figure out how to operate in this system. Be cute, be quiet, and keep to yourself.

By the time Joan came to me about thirteen-year-old Jill's drinking, the situation had become so exacerbated that I wasn't sure it could ever be straightened out. But Joan had hit bottom and was willing to do anything to have a happier homelife, so she began to tell the truth. She admitted that she missed working, that she had made Jill the scapegoat, that she had shortchanged Tom. She saw that to her, Hank was the goose that laid the golden eggs, and that she had been terrified of cutting off her supply. She also saw that her fear had immobilized her, keeping her trapped in an untenable situation. She saw that placing Sarah in the role of Perfect Child had in fact put tremendous burdens on Sarah, the very ones Joan had vowed never to impose on her own child. Joan realized all this and much, much more.

As she began to reveal these things to her family, there were some upsets. She declared she was going back to work part-time. Hank was shaken by this until he realized it was not personal. It was not a reflection on him as a provider, husband, lover, or father.

Joan also stopped blaming herself for Jill's drinking. She realized that the drinking might be symptomatic of alcoholism, the predisposition for which could have been transmitted genetically from Hank's father. She began to communicate directly with Jill about the drinking—without guilt. Soon the responsibility for Jill's behavior returned to its rightful owner—Jill.

As Jill and Joan began to develop an intimate relationship, Tom and Sarah felt left out. They formed a coalition, with their father, against Joan and Jill. But Joan didn't try to fix anything. She just kept revealing what was going on with her—without blaming anyone.

Tom tried a little rebelling (now that Jill had abdicated that post), but Sarah just became more and more perfect. Eventually, Hank came around. He saw how threatened he was, and how threatened Sarah was by all these changes. One day he sat down and talked with Sarah, perhaps for the first time ever. Slowly but surely, the barriers were breaking down. Intimacy was taking place in the Smith family.

I see them only occasionally now. Sometimes they revert to old patterns. That's not unusual. Robots are persistent. But the Smiths don't need much help getting out of these situations. They've moved all around the board, trading places and responsibilities. They've developed flexibility and the willingness to communicate directly. Intimacy has taken hold and they've experienced its benefits—closeness, comfort, and love. The chances of their seriously reverting to the old ways are very, very slim.

Family Dynamics

Everything in nature seeks balance, and families are no exception. Homeostasis is the process by which something finds internal stability and balance. The word comes from *homeo* (the same) and *stasis* (standing).

In families, homeostasis is the balance that results when each person plays his or her role. It prevents chaos and confusion, and gives the family a certain equilibrium, because everyone's responses are fairly predictable in any given situation.

Imagine a mobile, a perfectly balanced work of art.

Imagine that each element hanging from the mobile is one member of your family. If one person changes positions in the mobile, everyone else has to change position as well in order to maintain the balance. The mobile has to be flexible to make these changes and adjustments. If it is not flexible, it breaks. When the homeostasis in families becomes rigid, no one can move, grow, or express himself for fear of destroying the family.

When families feel threatened, the homeostasis is inclined to become more rigid. The threat might be internal (the discovery that one person is an alcoholic, or gay, or in some way unacceptable to society) or external (financial reversals, ethnic discrimination, or some other attack from the outside), but whenever the family feels it is in danger of being ostracized or broken apart, it will gather its forces and solidify the roles in an effort to protect itself and survive.

This is a natural thing for organisms to do. Our bodies do it all the time. If I get a little tear in my back muscle, all the muscles around it get hard and inflexible in order to protect that tear. The pain is so great I become incapacitated. Interestingly enough, my dysfunction comes not from the tear itself, but from all the other muscles locking into place around it in order to protect it.

This is exactly what happens with families. Sometimes we feel we need to lock into our roles during times of stress—but the sooner we can release that rigidity and return to a more flexible homeostasis, the better off we will be.

An upper-middle-class family I know was faced with just such a crisis when the youngest son, who was thirty, secretly became addicted to—and involved with dealing—cocaine. He was not only physically debilitated but being pursued by dealers to whom he owed money. He finally realized he had no alternative but to tell his family. They felt very threatened by the situation. Their first response was to jump into the roles they had played when the children were young. The father bailed his son out financially and gave him a good stiff lecture. The mother was utterly compassionate, holding him in her arms and wailing, "How could they do this to my baby?" The oldest daughter, who had been the Perfect Child, made arrangements for her brother to come stay with her and took care of everybody else. The middle son, the Rebel, made sure his brother got "alternative" forms of treatment.

At first glance, all this role-playing might not appear very healthy. But the fact is, that son needed someone to pay off the mob. He needed someone who just loved him and accepted him no matter what he had done. He needed a place to stay and a treatment program. If this family's rigid homeostasis had continued for years after the crisis, it might have led to some severe dysfunction. The father would have spent the rest of his life bailing out his son and delivering lectures. The mother might have coddled him to the point that he couldn't do anything for himself. The sister could easily have become a martyr and the new mother to the family. The middle son might have become a "co-addict," constantly pushing his brother into new treatment programs.

Fortunately, the entire family entered treatment and became more flexible, yet stronger, once the crisis had passed. And having weathered it together, their levels of intimacy increased appreciably. We need the protection that homeostasis gives us for a time, but at some point the rigidity needs to be released so that we can return to the flow of life. There is a give-and-take to the homeostasis in healthy families. People move freely in and out of various roles. The balance is always maintained, because no one is trapped in any particular place, and can move around to fill all the holes when they occur.

If the family roles don't return to a more fluid state once the crisis is over, people begin to think that those roles are who they are. They become trapped and nonadaptive. Movement stops, growth stops, flexibility stops. The entire organism becomes fixed. The family can't make its contribution to society, because it is so concerned with maintaining its protective dynamic.

Just as individuals want to protect their place in the family, the family wants to protect its place in society. When there is someone in the family who is an oddball or a black sheep, someone who might discredit the family in society, then the family with rigid homeostasis tries to hide that person, to change him, to deny that he exists, or to ostracize him. When the family's homeostasis is more flexible, they can make room for him, and everyone benefits.

Many of our society's greatest contributors have been rebels or "oddballs." Einstein and Churchill were slow learners who disliked their early schooling. Gaugin, Matisse, and Schweitzer left their families to pursue their work. Balanchine had five wives, and Freud was a heavy cocaine user. The list is endless.

In spite of their "different" natures, each of them made tremendous contributions to society. Had they been shackled by the constraints of normality, they might never have done so.

I'm not advocating that we urge our children to marry five times or use cocaine in order to be creative, but I do believe that somehow we must make room for the fact that people who are different often have a great deal to offer. If we can accept our "resident rebels" without allowing them to take control and make everyone miserable, I think they have a greater chance of expressing their "differences" in a healthy and productive way.

Any one person can shift the entire dynamic of a family at any time. Even if someone is away temporarily, their space must be filled. When I called home from a week-long business trip recently, my daughter Megan said, "Hurry home, Mom. Now that you're gone they're all teasing *me*!"

Homeostasis can see us through hard times and keep us on an even keel. But we have to be careful. If we depend on it too heavily, it becomes rigid and inflexible, and no longer serves us.

The Dysfunctional Family

Dysfunction means "impaired or abnormal functioning" or "a nonadaptive trait or condition, especially one failing to serve a useful or adjustive purpose in society."

In dysfunctional families, the survival of both the individual and the family depends on each individual becoming thoroughly identified with his role. The more fragile and threatened the family feels, the greater the investment it will require to keep people in their places and solidify their roles. This makes it impossible for people to see who they are beyond their roles in the family, and severely limits how much of themselves they can reveal.

Needless to say, intimacy is practically impossible under these circumstances. Not only do people lose sight of who they really are, but they can't tolerate other family members saying or doing things that might threaten their role. No one can make themselves known or allow others to make themselves known. Everyone's energy becomes focused on his or her own survival, and on the survival of the family, to the exclusion of growth, expression, self-discovery, and intimacy.

Families can become dysfunctional from many causes. Sometimes the threat is from the outside—economic reversals, natural disasters, a community that demands certain kinds of behaviors. More often, however, the perceived threat is from within the family. There may be "family secrets," "skeletons in the closet" that no one wants discovered, or simply a very low level of communication.

One family member might develop a chemical dependency, a disease or handicap of some sort, or simply be acting out problems that already exist in the family. This person can easily become the scapegoat for all the family's trouble. Every family has a scapegoat.

Some families are so tightly knit that they have to find their scapegoat *outside* the nuclear family—selfish old Aunt Suzie, Grandma, the Democrats, "the system." But when

the family's standing in the community is threatened from
the inside, family members are apt to deny that the problem
exists. If one family member's alcoholism begins to be apparent, for instance, the family may say, "Joe? Oh, no,
he's not an alcoholic. He drinks a little too much sometimes, but . . ." The family has to deny, even to itself, that
Joe has a problem with alcohol. If the community found
out, it might turn against them. The family must protect
itself against that at all costs, and the cost may be that Joe
never has a chance to acknowledge and deal with his alcoholism.

Let's look at how a dysfunctional situation can come
about. The Walters live in a Chicago suburb. Julie and John
have three children: Sally, sixteen; Tracy, fourteen; and Jack,
thirteen. Last winter, Julie began to suspect that Tracy was
abusing marijuana. She started coming home late, became
uncommunicative and irritable, missed school, and let her
grades fall. Occasionally, her eyes were red-rimmed and she
was becoming increasingly listless.

Julie mentioned her fears to John, but neither of them
knew exactly what to do, and so they didn't do much of
anything. Julie tried to work drug information into other
kinds of conversations with Tracy, but Tracy responded by
withdrawing to her room. That made Julie think she had
made a mistake, and so she stopped even this roundabout
communication.

At this point, the problem still seems minor. Analogous
to the situation with my back muscles, the strain is there, but
the muscle hasn't yet been torn. After all, the Walters have
no proof that Tracy is smoking dope. Maybe she's just ex-
hibiting the moods of a teenager. Still, everyone in the family
senses that something is changing, something is wrong, and
the tension is starting to build. Something is in the air, but
nobody's talking about it. They are not making their real
concerns known to one another.

Tracy's siblings, Sally and Jack, know that whatever the
problem is, it has to do with Tracy. Neither of them can resist

the temptation to take advantage of the situation and move into a better position in the family. Sally is the Perfect Child, and she starts to look better by the day. She pulls her B-pluses up to A's, makes the cheerleading squad, and even seems to help around the house more. Jack has been covering two bases—Loner and Charmer—but he's definitely leaning more toward the latter now. At this point, anyone who shows no signs of drug use is a joy to have around the Walters home. Sally and Jack seldom miss an opportunity to create whatever little irritations they can and make Tracy look even worse than she already does.

Julie and John's relationship is under some pressure, too. They feel frustrated, and blame themselves and one another for the rotten way they've raised this kid. Julie wants to be sympathetic, supportive, and reasonable. John says, "Ground her." All the muscles are starting to tighten, making it even more likely that the muscle will tear because of all the tension. Tracy just wants to get out of the house. She thinks the problem is her family.

Finally, Tracy gets arrested for shoplifting. The police find marijuana in one pocket and $1,500 in the other. Another kid tells the police that Tracy is not only using but dealing.

This is the crisis point, the tear. At this point, the Walters have an opportunity to become a truly functional family, or to become a truly dysfunctional family. They can go either way. What will determine their direction is their willingness or unwillingness to make known to themselves and one another what is going on, and to tell the truth about what is happening.

If they go the dysfunctional route, their Robots will take over and everyone will blame one another for Tracy's situation. Or they will put the blame outside the family—on the school system, the pediatrician who didn't tell them something, the grandmother, a congressional committee, Tracy's rotten friends, the hydrogen bomb, *anything*. Roles will become more fixed, and no one will dare rock the boat more by telling the truth.

Sally will have to be more perfect; Jack will try to gloss everything over with charm. Julie will cry, John will make sure Tracy gets a suspended sentence, and everyone will try to forget it ever happened. No one will want to talk about it; they will simply tighten the screws on themselves and one another.

The family may manage to limp along this way for a while. John and Julie may continue to go to work, the kids may continue to go to school, and somehow the earth will keep spinning. If that happens, and the family does in fact survive, everyone may decide that solidifying the roles and making the homeostasis more rigid was just the thing to do. They will do it again in the next crisis, and again and again until the family becomes completely dysfunctional, and no one can grow or be themselves. Tracy's problem—or some-one else's—will resurface, probably in an exaggerated form, and that may tear the family apart.

The alternative—the opportunity for true intimacy—is for the Walters to sit down, with a counselor if necessary, and make known to one another what their fears are about the family, what they think this represents to them, how they feel about Tracy and about themselves, and then decide what they want to do. They have an opportunity to talk to Tracy and tell her their concerns for her health and safety, and to listen to her. They can hear what she has to say about her problem, why she is using and dealing marijuana, and what she thinks she has to do in order to stop.

In the process, John and Julie will have to admit they have a child who is in trouble. They will have to confront their fears of being bad parents, and look at what they can do to support Tracy. Sally and Jack may have to let Tracy get more positive attention than they are right now, and to notice how that affects them.

None of this will be possible if people are letting their

Robots operate. It's going to require a leap of faith, a letting go of the old ways and the need to be "right." It's going to mean surrendering to the Spirit (although they probably wouldn't use that word), trusting themselves, and trusting Tracy. It may not be easy, but it will bring them a whole new way of relating to one another, to themselves, and to life.

There is a great deal of interest in dysfunctional families these days. Nearly everyone seems to have grown up in one, or to be *wondering* if they grew up in one. Making the judgment about whether or not a family is dysfunctional is a very subjective thing. Siblings may radically disagree about the state of the parent family. Christina Crawford wrote *Mommie Dearest* to convey what she perceived to be a thoroughly dysfunctional family, yet two of her siblings didn't agree at all with her observations.

Dysfunctional families usually have one or more members who are obviously impaired in some way. They may suffer from alcoholism, schizophrenia, or something as seemingly innocuous as workaholism. There may be violence in the house. Often the people in dysfunctional families simply feel cold and cut off. The most common kind of dysfunction is this emotional impairment, in which people don't feel whole and don't feel as if they are contributing either to the family or to the community. It's important to recognize that the dysfunction does not cause physiological conditions such as addiction, schizophrenia, or clinical depression, but it will exacerbate them. This is unfortunate, since the dysfunction often comes about as the result of the Robot's attempts to avoid the ramifications of these diseases.

Dysfunctional families approach life from the perspective of what they have to avoid, rather than from the perspective of growth, love, expression, and contribution. They live within their Robots, with little access to the Spirit.

If you are part of a dysfunctional family:

1. Remember that any one person can change the entire dynamic at any time, simply by stepping out of his or her role and creating a new model.

2. Remember that it does no good to blame the other family members. Consider that we often find ourselves in certain situations from which we can learn lessons, and on some level, you may have chosen these circumstances. Your Robot will want to blame them and say there is nothing you can do about your situation because the other people in your family will never change. The challenge is to move beyond your Robot into Spirit, and to create the kind of intimacy you want either with these people or with a new group who may be more inclined toward intimacy. Your Robot will have to give up being "right" about how awful your family is and how impossible it is for you to have intimacy because of them, but it will be well worth the discomfort.

A family's first experience with true intimacy represents a huge change in the homeostasis. In intimate relationships, everyone gets to reveal *all* of themselves—not just the roles—and to let others reveal themselves as well. This is sure to upset the applecart.

Intimacy always requires taking risks. The more taut the family's homeostasis, the greater the risk. If you are the person who introduces intimacy—or any other big change—you have to be prepared to take the blame for all the upheaval. The family's balance, and therefore its survival, have been threatened—and you are the one who is making waves. You have to be willing for your family to say the equivalent of "I'm sorry but you're a threat to us, and we don't want anything to do with you."

This is the challenge then—moving from survival into the Spirit. We have a higher purpose than survival. We are on earth to take the next evolutionary step, and that step is toward Spirit—toward self-discovery, love, and our higher power.

Family relationships are our greatest challenge and our greatest opportunity. They can be frustrating and painful, but they can also give us what nothing else can—ourselves and our connection with our higher power.

QUESTIONS TO ASK YOURSELF

What were the circumstances in my biological family?
How did I want it to be?
What role(s) did I play?
What role(s) do I play now in my biological family?
What role(s) do I play in my other relationships?
What was the dynamic in my family?
Who was the Perfect Child? The Rebel? The Loner? The
    Charmer?
Who plays those roles in my life outside my biological family?

THINGS TO DO

Draw a picture of the dynamic in your biological family (stick
    figures will do).
Find someone to share the picture with.
Ask that person to draw a picture of his or her family and
    to share the dynamic with you.

CHAPTER THREE

INTIMACY BY CHOICE

I've talked to many people who think that achieving intimacy is a matter of chance. You either have it in your relationships or you don't. If you're virtuous enough, or intelligent enough, or draw the right number in the cosmic lottery, then maybe intimacy will just fall into your lap. But maybe not.

I prefer to think of intimacy as a state of being we can choose, a context we can create. If intimacy is the willingness to make yourself known to others and to allow them to make themselves known to you, then it does become a matter of choice rather than of chance. Creating it may be risky or uncomfortable, but it is something that is available to all of us.

Intimacy is not a matter of biological chance; it is something that you choose and create. You can create intimacy in your biological family, or you can create intimacy in a "chosen" family. All it takes is the willingness to make yourself known and to let others make themselves known to you—and the courage to embrace what you discover about yourself and about others.

For Rosa and her mother, making themselves known to each other took them a long way toward intimacy. Rosa told me that she and her mother battled constantly over the fact that Rosa wasn't married. At thirty-two, Rosa was sick of being badgered and could hardly stand to talk with her mother on the phone, let alone travel to Arizona to see her. Each time her mother brought up the subject, Rosa would talk vaguely about men she was dating, or *make up* men she was dating, and then steered the subject away from marriage. When she hung up, she felt awful about herself and angry with her mother. She dreaded the next phone call and resented her mother for driving this wedge between them.

Rosa wasn't very optimistic about what would happen if she began making herself known to her mother, and letting her mother make herself known as well, but she decided that she could no longer take the relationship the way it was. She finally reached the point where she was willing to make a break with her mother if that was what happened when they talked honestly to one another.

The next time her mother called and started her third degree, Rosa said, "Mama, I hate it when you talk to me like that. Leave me alone; it's my life, and I'll live it any way I want."

Her mother replied, "I know it's your life, but I can't stand by and watch you ruin it!" It was Robots on parade, back and forth like this for the entire conversation, but something had changed. A layer of "politeness" had been shaken loose and there was room for some kind of communication. Even if Rosa and her mother were only revealing their Robots to one another, they were at least revealing *something*.

As time went on, they started to go beyond the Robots. Rosa could say, "When you say those things, I feel like I'm not okay with you because I'm not married. It hurts me because I want your love and your approval."

Her mother could tell Rosa that she *did* love her, and was afraid she'd been a bad mother because Rosa wasn't doing what all her friends' daughters were doing. She wanted the best for Rosa, and as far as she knew, being married was the best way to live. Each time they talked, Rosa and her mother saw a little more of the other's point of view and a little more of what was behind the other's words. And that, of course, was love. The conversations began moving away from "who they were not" and toward "who they were."

It was an uncomfortable process, because they had never done it before and they had to make themselves vulnerable to each other. They never did see exactly eye to eye, but they could talk honestly, relax and be themselves, remember that they loved each other, and even laugh at their ongoing "battle." Oddly enough, two years after these conversations began, Rosa got married. She didn't have to fight her mother's viewpoint anymore.

True intimacy means being willing to listen to the other person, to see things from his point of view for a moment, even if you don't agree with him. Easy to say, but when people hurt us, we have a natural tendency either to pull away from them or to fight back. "Flight or fight" is still a hormonal response, whether we like it or not. But we are, after all, still evolving. We're talking about moving from one level of existence to another. We no longer have bears chasing after us; the challenge now is to go beyond "flight or fight," beyond the Robot into Spirit.

Intimacy Can't Be Forced

You can't force or cajole someone into being intimate with you. If you try, you may get a lot of information about the person, but you won't get his essence. You may not even get the information. People are inclined to clam up when they feel intimacy being forced on them.

My client Ann learned this lesson in a memorable way. Ann's mother died when she was seven, and her father remarried a woman with two children. Ann never felt very good about her stepmother. She had adored her own mother, who was a warm and cuddly woman. Ann's stepmother was shy and somewhat aloof, but Ann decided she was downright unfriendly. This new woman was not her mother and was never going to *be* her mother. Ann shut her stepmother out and refused to relate to her. But she never faced the fact that she contributed to the coldness.

When Ann grew up, she married a man who was divorced and had two children. Ann wanted more than anything not to be "cold and unfeeling" like her own stepmother had been, so she set about creating this warm, cozy, intimate relationship with her new stepchildren.

They wanted no part of her, of course, just as she had wanted no part of her own stepmother. Ann couldn't understand this, because she was working so hard to be close to them. The more she tried to be intimate with these kids, the more they didn't want anything to do with her.

As we talked, Ann saw that by trying to force an intimate relationship on her stepchildren, she was actually creating more distance from them. She was trying to *be* their mother, and it was a relationship they didn't want. They already had a mother, and had been trying to tell her that in the only way they knew how—by staying remote from her and pushing her away. They had been trying to make themselves known, but she hadn't wanted to listen.

When Ann stopped trying to win their affection and force intimacy on them, things improved dramatically. She could let them know she cared about them, tell them which behaviors were acceptable to her and which weren't, and relate to them genuinely as people rather than as "child" and "mother." They felt a freedom to be themselves with her that they hadn't felt before. The relationships began to be based not on roles, but on human beings making themselves known to one another.

The First Step

If we are first fairly intimate with ourselves, we've already gone a long way toward intimacy with others. That means listening to ourselves and telling the truth. We're bound to hear things we don't like. If my identity is tied up in being a person who is kind and thoughtful, then at some point in an intimate relationship, I will probably have reactions that are not kind and thoughtful. Every person alive has moments when he is not *something* that he wants to be, and all these "negative" traits are likely to appear in the course of intimacy. In the process of revealing them to another person, they will also be revealed to *me*. I may not want to see them, but I have to include them as part of myself if I ever want to be intimate with anyone.

In an intimate relationship, we're constantly presented with the opportunity for greater self-acceptance. We might have finally become willing to reveal to ourselves that we're alcoholic, or selfish, or unreasonable. We think, "I've come to terms with that. I can handle it." But when we let that be known in the world, other people's reactions throw us for a loop. If people put us down, we can't handle it.

My client Don had been in his father's printing business for ten years when he saw that it wasn't what he wanted to do with his life. He had always wanted to be a painter, and when he turned thirty, he realized that if he didn't do it now, he would probably never do it. He realized there would be some problems when he told his parents and brother, who was also in the business, but he expected that those problems would blow over fairly quickly and that his family would ultimately support him in doing what he wanted to do.

Don was wrong. His father told him he was a bum and a traitor who belonged out on the street, where he would probably wind up anyway. His mother said Don had broken her heart and that he was to blame for his father's recent chest pains. His brother called him a pansy and an irresponsible ingrate. Don was outraged. He couldn't believe that anyone, especially his family, could be so narrow-minded and selfish, so unconcerned about his happiness. He felt maligned, betrayed, and cast out by the very people whose support he had counted on in this difficult time of transition.

This conversation went on for several months. Don didn't see any way he could ever connect with his family again without knuckling under and going back to the business, which he wasn't about to do, especially after their reaction.

The first thing Don had to realize in order to start healing the situation was that each of the other family members felt threatened in his or her own way, and they were just trying to protect themselves from hurt. All the Robots were operating in high gear. His father felt that Don was rejecting his life's work—and him—by leaving the business. His mother was frightened not only for her husband but for Don's well-being and financial security, and for the preservation of her family. His brother had had thoughts about leaving, too, but hadn't given himself permission to do it. Don's decision threatened everyone's self-esteem and identity in one way or another.

And on another level, everyone was worried about Don. A painter!? If he had said he wanted to be a corporate raider or a market analyst, they might have had a different reaction, but they didn't see how a painter could earn a living. Unfortunately, they didn't have access to the parts of themselves that could convey their real feelings to Don and let him know that their reactions came out of love for him. They just wanted to force him to come around to their point of view. To let him go ahead and live his own life, to do the thing that would make him happy, would have felt like an abdication of everything they stood for and everything they believed to be "right"—for themselves and for Don.

Don began to see himself as the martyr, the white knight who was just trying to discover and express his talents. Another part of him began to take his family's point of view, to castigate himself for causing all this trouble and being a bad son.

Don had to let go of these notions of "right" and "wrong." He had to stop thinking of himself as either the martyr or the bad son and realize that he was neither. He was just a man who had made a choice that happened to hurt his family, and they had struck back. He, in turn, had struck back at them, and that was going to have to stop if he was ever going to reconnect with them.

Don had believed that he had come to terms with his decisions and therefore could make himself known to them. What he *hadn't* been prepared for was their making themselves known to *him*.

Intimacy Begins Unilaterally—or, "You Go First"

So Don also had to take that next step toward self-acceptance and acceptance of others. He had to be true to himself without blaming them for blaming *him*. That didn't seem fair, but sometimes the first steps toward intimacy have to be unilateral. One person has to take the lead and step out of his Robot, whether or not anyone else follows suit.

Once Don could do that, once he could sit and listen to his family talk without reacting defensively or submitting to their point of view, some form of intimacy could begin. When they could express their negative reactions without resistance from Don, his father, mother, and brother had "room" to look past their original positions. Now they could begin to be aware of the feelings behind the accusations and what their real intentions were.

It wasn't easy for Don, but in the process he learned a lot about where his triggers and defenses were, and about his ability to move from the Robot into Spirit. He still got triggered from time to time, but he could see that it was just his Robot trying to protect itself. Don also learned a lot about his motivations for becoming a painter.

Don's family never approved of his new career, even after he had some success, but at least they could talk and make themselves known with one another. He could speak the truth about what he felt, and listen behind their words to what they were trying to tell him. It wasn't an ideal situation, perhaps, but it was one from which everyone had grown.

So what does Don do now that he's talking to his family, but not really experiencing much support? He's done the best he can with intimacy. He knows he loves his family and they love him, but he doesn't find much satisfaction in his relationships with them. They are more open now, but they rarely miss an opportunity to lash out at him—especially now that they know just where Don's vulnerable spots are.

Fortunately, Don's biological family is not his only option.

Choices

If Don is not getting his human need for love and support fulfilled in his biological family, and if they continue to make sarcastic remarks about his career at every opportunity, at some point it becomes appropriate for him to look around among the other people in the world and start creating a family of his own choosing.

Of course, not everyone who creates a "chosen" family does so because of a rift with his or her biological family. Sometimes family members live great distances from one another, and even though they are close emotionally, everyone feels the need to have a family close by. Sometimes family members die, or simply grow apart. Sometimes people get divorced, or never marry.

But our intense loyalty to our biological families, stemming no doubt from our original need for survival, nourishes us even when greatly strained. We are often willing to put up with more abuse from family members than we would from friends or acquaintances. We are probably willing to risk more and pay a higher price for intimacy. They are the people we are most likely to love; it makes sense to give intimacy our best shot with them.

Still, being related to a group of people by blood does

not ensure intimacy. And even when intimacy is achieved in the sense that Don did, where people are simply telling the truth about where their Robots are and making their judgments known to one another, we sometimes want or need more. We want to tell the truth, but we also want people in our lives who are willing to look at their Robot-like behavior, move beyond it, *share* the growing process. We want people who support us in our own growth whether or not they happen to agree with us. Because families are by nature oriented toward need and survival, because we have such high expectations of families, this kind of support isn't always available in our biological families.

Need spells disaster in relationships. This is one reason it takes so long to resolve parent-child relationships. There is such a high level of need involved. For many years, children truly needed their parents for physical and economic survival. By the time children are eighteen and ready to leave the nest, they have invested so much energy in the relationship with their parents that it can take years to undo any damage. It's not anybody's fault; it's just what happens when survival is a factor in a relationship.

When my friend Ruth went to Alcoholics Anonymous, she felt a sense of family and of intimacy that she'd never experienced with her own biological family. The particular homeostasis in her own family had, in fact, been detrimental to her. It was an environment in which she found it very hard not to drink. Ruth had to sever the connection with her family until she had a few years of sobriety and felt confident that she could go back and use what she had learned about intimacy in her AA family to reestablish the connection with her biological family.

There are families that absolutely refuse to accept certain behaviors or ways of being; families that, no matter what the "problematic person" does, continue to tell him he's no good, useless, wrong. There is a limit to how much of this any person can take. Even if he can take a lot, he probably needs some kind of support outside the family to see him through.

Once you let your family reveal themselves, you are in a position to make some choices. You can choose whether you want to keep them as your primary support group, whether you want to have them in your life on a limited basis, or whether you want to break the connection entirely. There are some relationships that we want to stay in no matter what, and others that we don't. It may be a difficult choice, but at least all the cards are on the table after everyone has made himself known. You don't have to wonder where people stand, or hide anything yourself.

Sometimes we get the idea that intimacy with our biological family is better than intimacy with a group we have created. That is not necessarily true. We have an unlimited capacity for love if we choose to draw from it. Our families afford us certain unique experiences, but that doesn't mean our love and our ability to be intimate are limited to those people.

Letting Go of Barriers

For me, family means support, commitment, contribution, and growth. But at the bottom of everything is love. We all want to love and be loved, and we spend a lot of time and energy *looking* for love. I believe that we all already *do* love one another and that certain things get in the way of our *experiencing* that love.

Ironically, the things that get in the way are things we do to *get* love. Love already exists for all of us. What blocks the experience of that love is our trying so hard to get it. For example, we usually criticize others "out of love." We want to love them, but there is one little thing that's in the way— a certain behavior or habit, or maybe just that they remind us of Aunt Agnes, whom we didn't like. If they would get rid of that one thing, then we could feel the love we have for them. Whenever something blocks our experience of loving another person, we criticize that thing because we want so badly to love that person.

Conversely, when we are criticized, we think people don't love us. If we deny that criticism or defend ourselves against it, the people who are criticizing us don't feel heard. Now they feel compelled to keep at it. If we can hear them, and remember that they love us, then they can move beyond it to the things they like about us.

Norma and her mother, Nellie, came to see me because they "just couldn't communicate" with each other.

As I observed them interact, it became clear that nothing Norma did was good enough for Nellie. Norma didn't sit right, talk right, wear her hair right, have the right job, raise her kids right. Not surprisingly, Norma was hypersensitive to the slightest indication of criticism—from Nellie or anyone else.

Norma and Nellie each had the "solution" to the problem. Norma just wanted Nellie to stop criticizing her and Nellie just wanted Norma to get her act together and do things "right." Each felt strongly that everything would be fine if the other would just change!

It took several sessions to convince them that requiring the other to change was not going to work.

I began seeing them separately, and bluntly told Norma that it was up to her to begin the shift. To Nellie, I said the same thing.

Norma felt criticized, of course. She thought I meant she had to change and do what her mother wanted. I clarified what I meant, which was simply for Norma to begin to hear her mother's criticisms, rather than rise up in defensive outrage at every comment. She choked at the suggestion, but tried it anyway.

Over time she became able to say things like, "Thanks, Mom, I appreciate your concern," or "I'm glad you told me how you feel." She was surprised she could do it, but even more surprised at her mother's reaction. Slowly but surely,

Nellie became less and less critical—and Norma never changed a thing other than her reaction. But now that Nellie was given space for her criticisms, she could get past them to her true experience, which was love and concern for her daughter.

In the meantime, I explained to Nellie that I understood that her comments were her way of expressing her love, but that Norma couldn't always see it that way. I told her that Norma was going to bristle at times, that Nellie should expect it and try not to get too upset about it.

I also suggested that she not let every little comment slip out of her mouth, that maybe every other one was enough. Nellie was able to laugh at that idea and gave it her best effort. She made the attempt and Norma appreciated it. For the first time in her life she actually felt her mother's love.

They still have conflicts, but having experienced their love for one another, they now feel complete. Norma is less and less attracted to critical people, because she's not obsessed with unfinished business with her mother, and Nellie feels like the loving mother she always wanted to be. At age sixty-eight she says it's better late than never.

So intimacy is the expression of the love and connection that already exist, not the struggle to get it. It has less to do with the subjects we discuss than it does with our emotional state. You don't have to talk about every detail of your life in order to be intimate with someone. I have an intimate relationship with my ninety-year-old aunt, but we've never discussed her sex life with Uncle George or mine with my husband. Being willing to be open and vulnerable, to reveal the truth as you see it, and to hear other people's truths may bring forth information, but it's the emotional openness, and not the information, that creates intimacy.

Intimacy is a natural state, just as love is a natural state. Attaining it is a matter of discovering and letting go of the barriers to the love and intimacy that already exist.

My client Betty discovered how artificial the barriers to love and intimacy are. Her 1940s marriage with her husband,

Fred, was traditional: She was the homemaker and he was the breadwinner. There was little real communication or intimacy in their relationship.

At the age of twenty-three, one of their daughters contracted leukemia and died. Betty and Fred rallied around each other in this tragedy and became very open and vulnerable. This was the first experience of real intimacy for both of them, and Betty realized how important it was to her.

As the months passed after their daughter's death, Fred fell back into the old patterns and began to close off. He had let himself be known, but there came a point when he said, "That's enough." He began to retreat into a position of self-protection. This was very difficult for Betty, especially after this brief but powerful experience of intimacy. She realized that she wanted intimacy in her life and that she was unlikely to get it with him, and so they divorced.

Betty's new relationships began with wonderful experiences of intimacy, but as soon as she heard something she didn't like about the person, the relationship would end. She would throw the baby out with the bathwater.

When she began to see that fostering intimacy meant letting others make themselves known to her, and her being able to respond to that knowledge honestly, things began to change. She met a man she liked, and one of the first things he did was suggest they get season football tickets. Normally, that would have ended the relationship, because Betty thought football was disgusting. Instead, she took a deep breath and said, "You know, I've always thought that people who liked football were brutes, but you're not a brute so I may have had a mistaken idea about that. I don't really enjoy football, but I think it would be great if you got tickets with someone else—preferably male. Then when you get back from the games we can go out to dinner and you can tell me all about it."

That way her friend remained who he was, a football fan, and she remained who she was, *not* a football fan, and they didn't have to end the relationship. We often wait for the other person to give us permission to be ourselves; it's important to remember that the permission doesn't come from them, but from us. Betty is finding out quite a bit about herself, and about intimacy, in this relationship. They don't have nearly as much in common as she expected, but she's getting wonderful practice at letting him reveal himself to her and revealing herself to him. She's finding out that what she really wanted was not her pictures of intimacy—the cozy togetherness she grew up with—but the opportunity to discover and to be herself.

Is It Worth It?

For me, it is. The most uncomfortable things about intimacy are also the things I value most. Those things include:

- Discovering parts of me I don't like

- Discovering parts of me I do like

- Hearing how you really feel about me, good or bad

- Learning how I really feel about you, good or bad

- Experiencing new emotions

- Telling the truth

When I make myself known to others and they make themselves known to me, things may arise that make one or both of us want to end the relationship. But if our connection was held together by lies or untold truths, how good was it?

I also find out things about myself that I don't particularly like, but those things were just beneath the surface anyway, festering because I wasn't dealing with them. Bringing them out in the open gives me power over them, and they no longer have to run my life. Letting go of them lets me love the people I want to love. I wouldn't trade intimacy for anything, because it gives me the ability to love. And love connects me with my higher power and, thus, to the purpose of my life.

QUESTIONS TO ASK YOURSELF

With whom in your biological family are you now intimate (or at least able to be genuine)?

With whom would you like to be more intimate?

What are you willing to do to create intimacy with those people?

What are your fears about creating intimacy with those people?

What do you need to communicate to these people?

THINGS TO DO

Call the people you would like to be close to, or send them a card. Connect with them in some way at least once a week for the next two months.

Write a list of the reasons you want to be more intimate with them.

Write a list of the reasons you can't be closer to them. Rip this list up and throw it away.

CHAPTER FOUR

INTIMATE COMMUNICATION

Robot or Spirit?

If intimacy involves making ourselves known to others and allowing others to make themselves known to us, then communication is vital to true intimacy. Our ability to communicate has a tremendous impact on our ability to be intimate. There are certain types of communication that promote intimacy, and others that do not.

According to Webster's, communication is "the giving, or the giving and receiving, of information as by talk, gestures, writing, etc." We are all communicating all the time, whether or not we realize it. We are sending messages to other people, and they are sending messages to us. We send information through words, facial expressions, tone of voice, body language, and even silence. The way we sit or stand, the clothing we wear, the "presence" we project—all these things are forms of communication. There is no such thing as "no communication"; there are only *unreceived* communications.

Communication is not necessarily a two-way street. We

can give messages that are not received, and we can fail to receive messages that other people give. Communication becomes more intimate as we become more sensitive to the messages others are sending us, and as we start sending our own messages in ways that are most likely to be received.

On some level, we transmit to others everything we are and everything we experience. People respond to these things, whether or not they are consciously aware of doing so. How often have you heard someone say one thing, but had the gut feeling that he meant just the opposite? Or just looked at another person and knew everything he or she was feeling?

The more I know about myself, the clearer I can be in my communication. I begin to notice when I am sending the message "Don't open up to me," or when I'm trying to sound very rational but am actually doing my best to make the other person "wrong" so I can be "right." Part of achieving intimacy is the ability to know when I am being defensive, when I am sending mixed messages, or when I'm acting from a particular prejudice or judgment—and to tell the truth about it.

In the path of intimate communication stands the Robot, who often wreaks havoc. Remember, the Robot bases its survival on past experiences. The Robot insists on knowing how things are. It doesn't like surprises. The Robot wants to be right, at all costs. It may think it wants intimacy, but intimacy means telling the truth, in the present. It requires the willingness to relinquish the concepts of right and wrong. It means welcoming the unknown.

Communication is the means to intimacy, and intimacy is terribly threatening to the Robot. Remember, the Robot's stock-in-trade is judgments and decisions that protect its position—two prime barriers to intimacy.

The Robot's decisions and judgments will always exist, but they don't have to control our behavior or determine who we are. The fact that my Robot has judgments, decisions, and prejudices does not mean that I am a prejudiced person; it just means I *have* certain judgments, decisions, and prejudices. I don't have to become identified with them. If I can let them surface and admit that I have them, I can then choose whether or not I want to act on them. They don't have to run me. When I try to hide them, even from myself, they persist and become stronger and, on some level, I begin to fear that I *am* them. *Having* judgments and decisions doesn't make me a bad person; it just means I'm human.

When I first discovered that I was an alcoholic, it became my whole identity. I *was* an alcoholic, rather than being a person who *had* the disease of alcoholism, but who had many other qualities as well. I approached people from a rather defensive posture: "I'm an alcoholic and what are you going to do about it?" I suppose I needed that defense when I first stopped drinking, but after a while it began to limit my relationships with people. Now I often make known to people that I have alcoholism, but it is not the basis of our relationship. Alcoholism is a disease I have, not who I am. By the same token, the Robot's decisions, judgments, and prejudices are things we *have*, not who we are. Only when we resist having them do they become problematic.

We can take back their power simply by *noticing* them, telling the truth about them, and choosing whether or not we want to act on them. When I talk about "noticing" the Robot's judgments and decisions, I don't mean evaluating them, judging them, justifying them, or rationalizing them. I mean just noticing them. That puts you in control. It means that you can let go of them. Even if you choose not to let go of them, you can tell the truth about them—to yourself and other people. When you do that, it will be easier for other people to do the same.

Communication starts with the process of becoming known to yourself. The Robot's judgments and decisions attempt to censor how you see the world. If your Robot has decided all men are one way and all women are another way, it won't want you to see individual men or women as different from those notions. That will severely limit both your experience of life and your ability to be intimate.

Of course, other people are walking around with *their* Robots censoring *their* experience, too. Nothing triggers a Robot so much as another Robot. When Robots do battle, it usually ends in a deadlock, with both struggling to be "right" and emerge from the situation as winners. This deadlock doesn't make anybody very happy, because ultimately no one wants to remain identified with the Robot.

For true communication and intimacy to exist, someone has to recognize that the Robots have taken over, then step back from the situation and listen from Spirit. When you step out of your own Robot, you can usually see how the other person's Robot got triggered. You understand that the other person is trying to protect himself, is acting out old patterns, and that the only way for him to move beyond his Robot is for you to stop fighting him.

When you are in Spirit, love comes through. You know the other person is hurt and defensive, you see all his human frailties, but you also see Spirit within him. He senses that on some level, and it makes it easier for him to see himself as lovable, which is probably all he wants.

This is key to intimate communication. Moving from Robot into Spirit is forgiving ourselves for being human, forgiving others for being human, and being willing to move out of old defensive patterns and habits into the love that exists naturally among all of us.

Sometimes people say, "Yes, but they really *were* wrong. Let me tell you what they did. . . ." From your Robot's point of view, the other person will *always* be wrong. People will always make mistakes, cause trouble, and act out all sorts of human weaknesses. The thing to remember is that your Robot is going nowhere with this kind of communication, and you have something available to you other than the Robot. You have your choice: You can be "right" or you can have intimacy.

Addiction to Nonintimate Communication

Nonintimate communication can be an addiction. I have seen many parallels between addiction to Robot communication and addiction to substances.

Research shows that alcoholics actually function better after a drink or two, up to a certain point in the progression of the disease, and that cigarette smokers function better mentally when they smoke.

There comes a point in every addiction, of course, when the substance causes people to function at much lower levels than they would if they had never used the substance, but people rarely recognize that point when they reach it. At the very least, people believe that without the substance or behavior, they would function *worse*. That is why they persist: They are afraid they will lose what they have, even if what they have is getting smaller by the day because of the addiction.

The co-addict is the person who makes it easier for the addict to get more addicted to his substance or behavior by protecting him from the consequences. The "co" is the wife who calls in sick for her husband when he's been on a bender, the child who makes sure the house is spotless so no one will notice her mother has been drunk all day, the man who puts up with his wife snorting coke because she feels so awful without it. "Co's" are addicts, too. They are addicted to the relationship with the addict. No matter how bad the relationship is, they figure that life would be worse without it and that the relationship itself would be worse if the addict were without his behavior or substance.

Superficially, they may be right. If you take a drug away from someone while that drug is still making him feel better instead of worse, there will be trouble. He will be cranky, irritable, confused, even violent, and his Robot will blame the people around him—especially the "co." On some level, the "co" knows this.

These same principles hold true for addiction to nonintimate communication. Politeness, good manners, and civility were developed to ease social tensions among people. When we have certain accepted and proscribed ways of relating and behaving, we don't have to think about what the truth is, what we feel, or what we really want the other person to know. These things probably wouldn't be "appropriate" topics of conversation anyway. We can operate "on automatic." The parameters of politeness and acceptability change with time, and from culture to culture, but they usually provide barriers to intimacy if people choose to use them.

We stay within the confines of nonintimate communication because we're afraid that if we don't, things will get worse. On the surface, they *may* get worse. If we admit to jealousy, we may be chided or put down. If we admit to anger, there might be a terrible fight. Things may look worse initially, but telling these uncomfortable truths opens up the possibility of moving beyond them. The distinction is whether we are taking responsibility for these feelings or blaming them on the other person. If we are taking responsibility, there will be an end to the fight, an end to the anger and a reconciliation based on honesty. Those things aren't possible if the anger is never experienced or expressed.

Patterns of nonintimate communication can be just as difficult to break as addictions. They are habits of long standing, and from time to time they have actually worked for us. Someone might say, "You don't know my father. I could never tell him that. He'd fly off the handle and never speak to me again. It would really make things worse." That sounds reasonable, and there may be some truth to it. Risk is definitely present in intimate communication, but if that risk is not taken, the situation will become deadlocked and eventually get much worse than we can imagine.

We are all afraid of losing something—a relationship, self-esteem, respect for ourselves, security, whatever—and that is why it is so difficult to shift our behaviors. We have survived the way things are; if we start revealing ourselves, all our "negative" traits may come to the surface and we don't know what would happen then.

Sometimes we are simply not willing to do it, and sometimes other people aren't willing to do it, either. No matter how much we love the alcoholic, no matter how much we make ourselves known, no matter what we do, we cannot make him stop drinking if he doesn't want to stop. He has to make that choice for himself.

The same is true of nonintimate communication. Some people are just not willing to give it up. We can create intimacy for ourselves by making ourselves known and providing an environment in which others can do the same, but we can't make them reveal themselves to us. The irony is that, in protecting ourselves from knowing and revealing things we don't like about ourselves, we often lose everything anyway.

I once worked with an alcoholic, Ray, who had stopped drinking, but was not in any sort of recovery program and had little interest in dealing with his past or even communicating about it. He just wanted to forget about all the anger and violence that had been in his life when he was drinking. He refused to tell his daughter, Martha, even when she started showing signs of alcoholism. She wanted desperately to be close to him, but his communication with her was so minimal that she didn't even know he was an alcoholic.

That was fine with Ray's wife. She thought alcoholism was a character fault, rather than the disease we now know it to be, and didn't want to hear about his drinking or his violence. She was just glad he had stopped, and didn't want to talk about it.

Martha completely denied her alcoholism. She couldn't see that it might be responsible for her mood swings and the trouble she was having with her parents. I couldn't tell her that her father was an alcoholic—which made it much more likely that she would have the disease—because he had talked to me in confidence.

I didn't see Martha for about a year, and then I learned that she had committed suicide. If she had been aware of Ray's alcoholism, she might have been able to recognize her own and do something about it. If they had been able to reveal more of themselves to one another, the suicide might have been avoided. Ray wasn't willing to do that. He had too much invested in "saving face."

In this situation, everyone was doing the best he or she could not to make things worse. But in the end, their unwillingness to reveal themselves just led to more isolation and fear. Ray was afraid of losing Martha's respect. She was afraid of losing his, and her own. The mother was afraid to consider the fact that Martha might be an alcoholic, because then she would have raised a child with a character defect.

The reason no one communicated intimately was that they were all terrified of what they would find out about themselves and have to reveal to one another. In their efforts to keep things from getting any worse, they all contributed to the worst possible outcome.

Guidelines for Intimate Communication

The only thing necessary to break the pattern of nonintimate communication is the willingness to reveal ourselves—our Spirits as well as our Robots—and to let others do the same. These are some exercises designed to get beyond the Robot to intimate communication:

1. *Watch out for "stuffing" and "dumping."* These may sound like basketball phrases, but they are two of the Robot's favorite techniques.

Stuffing means keeping the lid on your emotions. The Robot does this because it doesn't want to look bad, and is so skillful that you sometimes don't even know those feelings are there. As children, we are taught that some kinds of emotions are acceptable and some are not. You can cry at movies, but not at your birthday party. You can't act disappointed if you don't like Uncle Charlie's Christmas present. We learn to stuff down feelings that make us, or others, uncomfortable. As we grow older, we use stuffing to hide other kinds of emotions, aspects of ourselves that we don't like and don't want other people to see.

Elinor was taught that nice little girls don't get angry. She learned to stuff her anger as a child, and that worked pretty well for her Robot. It knew that people didn't like anger in adults any better than they liked it in children. Anger was definitely "wrong," and her Robot wanted above all else to be "right." So Elinor never ever got angry.

This kind of behavior takes its toll, not just on our psyche but on our bodies. Beyond that, it can't be maintained indefinitely. At some point, all that unexpressed anger is going to come surging out—usually in the most inappropriate places and at the most awkward times. Like a volcano when it is ready to erupt, there isn't much we can do about it. These unexpected eruptions make us look far worse than we would look if we released the anger as it came up.

Elinor's volcano erupted one afternoon with her kids. She had had a terrible day. Her boss had gotten angry at her for something she didn't do, and Elinor just sat there quietly explaining her point of view, which didn't convince him. She needed her job, so she stuffed her anger. On the bus coming home, some teenagers with a huge radio pushed her out of the way and got the last seats. Elinor was furious, but was afraid of confronting the kids—so she stuffed her anger again.

By the time she got home, Elinor was exhausted from holding in her anger. When she walked in the door, the kitchen looked like a disaster area. The kids had been fixing an after-school treat of peanut butter and jelly sandwiches. Now they were running around the house letting off steam. It was too much for her, and she exploded. She yelled and screamed as she never had before, blamed them for making her life miserable, gave them all a good smack, and sent them to their rooms. They were astonished and terrified. They had never seen this part of their mother before.

What Elinor did with her children is called "dumping." Dumping is letting your Robot run wild, spewing out emotions, judgments, and punishments without any awareness or acknowledgment that it is just your Robot. Dumping usually happens as a result of stuffing. The emotion being stuffed feels like anger, but it really is a feeling of powerlessness which then creates the experience of anger. Research by Carol Tarvis disputes the long-held belief that anger needs to be "vented." In fact, venting anger only makes one more hostile.

The ways to deal with anger are threefold: (1) finding a way to confront the situation, (2) communicating directly about it, and (3) having some understanding of the other's viewpoint so that you don't take the situation personally. Otherwise, all the pent-up emotion comes rushing out without any effort at responsible communication.

If Elinor had become aware that she was stuffing, and then been able to acknowledge and deal with her powerlessness, she might have been able to reveal it appropriately. If she had been dealing with it over the past thirty years, she wouldn't have been so angry at her boss. If she had been willing to communicate with her boss, she wouldn't have been so angry at the kids on the bus. If she hadn't been so upset by the kids on the bus, the boss, and the last thirty years, she wouldn't have dumped all her anger on her children. Instead, she might have been able to say, "Look, I've just had the worst day of my life, and I come home to a mess in the kitchen and you guys screaming all over the house. It's more than I can handle right now, so I'm going to yell at you for twenty seconds and then I want you to clean up the kitchen and go outside to play."

Making yourself known to someone is not the same as dumping. It's not the same as whining, griping, and complaining. Those things don't create intimacy; they create distance. What creates intimacy is looking deeper to see what triggered your Robot into action, and then telling the truth about it in a way that doesn't blame the other person or create the expectation that he has to fix things for you.

Fran was going through a difficult period in her life.

She was having trouble getting a job, her boyfriend just broke up with her, her car needed a new transmission, and the washing machine had broken down in midcycle. Fran headed straight for the phone and called her mother—collect. She spent the next half hour full of self-pity, whining and complaining. Her attitude was also defensive, because she thought her mother's response to her situation should be to send money, but she also knew her mother was probably too selfish to do that.

When Fran dumped all this in her mother's lap, she wasn't really making herself known. She was making her Robot known, and then not taking the next step and acknowledging that this was only her Robot, that she was going through a hard time and just wanted to tell someone all the reactions her Robot was having. If she had truly made herself known, Fran might have said, "I've just hit bottom today and need to tell somebody about it. I feel like God is mistreating me and I can't do anything right. I know it's not anybody's fault, but I'm really feeling sorry for myself and this is how I feel. . . ." She could say she felt like a poor, mistreated creature as long as she made it clear that she knew that's not who she really was, and that she didn't expect her mother to do anything about it. It's one thing to say you *feel* abused and mistreated; it's quite another to adopt the point of view you really *are*. The trick is not just to say that your feelings are not you, but to recognize that they truly aren't.

Thus, the antidote to dumping and stuffing is to recognize your emotions as they come up and communicate about them responsibly—that is, letting people know that these are just your Robot's reactions to certain situations. They don't make you "right," and they don't make the other person "wrong." They are just what is up for you right now, and you want to express them so you can let go and get on to the next thing.

2. *Don't justify your responses.* If I notice four black teenage boys coming toward me laughing and playing a radio at full blast, I may have an inclination to cross the street. If that's the case, I may have to acknowledge to myself that I have certain prejudices or belief systems about black teenage boys who swagger and play loud music.

I *have* those things, but they are not who I am. Unless I realize that, I may feel that I have to justify my response. If I am afraid of *being* a prejudiced person, rather than simply *having* a prejudice, I will want to justify and rationalize my reaction by saying something like, "Well, it's a fact that the crime rate for blacks is very high, and teenage boys of any race are known to be violent and troublesome."

Justifying my Robot's reaction only gives it more power and keeps me stuck. If I just admit that it exists, even if I don't like it, then I can choose to act on it or not. I can cross the street or stay where I am, and neither choice makes me a bad or a good person. To avoid justifications and rationalizations, I have to be in communication with myself. I have to be aware of what is going on with me and tell the truth about it.

3. *Be aware of payoffs and hidden agendas.* A payoff is some benefit the Robot derives from certain types of communication. Elaine knew that her husband, Roger, became violent and sometimes hit her when he was angry. She came to me wondering whether or not to leave him. I asked her to identify the occasions on which he got angry, and at first it seemed that most of the time it was just out of the blue.

But when I asked what happened after he hit her and the anger had passed, Elaine said he was profusely apologetic. He begged her forgiveness and would do anything for her. She began to see that her payoff was getting him just where she wanted him, groveling around and willing to do anything she asked. Elaine's hidden agenda was to get Roger under control. She was willing to be battered for that payoff.

Elaine saw how she had participated in this dynamic, and she stopped provoking him intentionally. At the same time, she saw that she did not want to live under the same roof with someone who beat her under *any* conditions. Fortunately, Roger went into therapy to look at his own patterns and payoffs and there have been no more violent incidents.

Hidden agendas are the secret plans the Robot develops in order to manipulate others, look good, and be "right." When I am communicating with someone, it helps to have some sense of what my true motives are. It also helps to distinguish those true motives from my *apparent* motives and from what I *wish* my motives were.

If I feel inadequate or stupid, my hidden agenda might be to put you down in our communication. The payoff would be that I looked smart and you looked stupid. Payoffs and hidden agendas can get you some small measure of control, but they will never bring about intimacy.

4. *Listen to yourself.* Hear what you are saying, as well as what others are saying. Learn to recognize when the speaker is the Robot, and when it is the Spirit. Be willing to hear and tell the truth about decisions, judgments, opinions, and other barriers to intimacy. The better you can hear yourself, the more quickly you can distinguish between the Robot and the Spirit, and the more quickly you can establish intimacy.

If I hear myself calling people "selfish" a lot, I may be looking in a mirror. The frequency with which I use that word should be a clue to me that I'm feeling very self-concerned lately and don't particularly like it, so I'm projecting it onto other people.

Listen to the words you use and to the types of statements you make. Do you use the word "you" more than "I"? Do you cloak judgments in statements of fact?

We have to be able to hear our own messages before we can hear what others are saying.

5. *Let go of the need to be "right" and to win at another's expense.* The Robot will always feel this need, but you don't have to be a slave to it. People spend unbelievable amounts of time and energy arguing about whether something happened on Tuesday or Wednesday, whether the sweater was blue or red, whether Aunt Suzie or Uncle Henry dented the fender—things that make absolutely no difference in the larger scheme of things.

Some people think their opinion is the only one that's worth considering, because they've thought it out so carefully. Others adopt a moral stance. They don't care what other people think or feel; their way is "right" and any other way is "wrong." They have to stand by their position no matter what, even if it costs them a relationship, because they believe that if they aren't "right," then they will be "wrong."

These people refuse to believe that there is no right or wrong, that there is just my experience, and your experience, and their experience, and everybody else's experience. None of these is the truth; they are all just experiences. They say, "But I *am* right. I have more expertise in this area," and refuse to recognize that other people's experiences are just as valid as theirs.

6. *Practice moccasin walking.* As one wise Indian said, "Never judge another man until you have walked two miles in his moccasins." The way I illustrate moccasin walking in workshops is to have two people sit facing one another. I ask one to describe the room he sees as if it is all he has ever seen or heard about. I then ask the other to do the same thing. One might see a wall of windows with trees outside, a pile of pillows, and some chairs stacked against the wall. The other might see a group of people, a blackboard, and a podium. They are in the same room, but they see it from two different points of view. Then I ask them to change seats and repeat the exercise, to walk in one another's moccasins.

Moccasin walking is recognizing that we see the room from different angles, and that your experience is just as valid for you as mine is for me. No one is "right" or "wrong"; we just have different points of view. Acceptance of another's point of view doesn't mean capitulation. It just means that you have your point of view and the other person has his, and there is no need for anyone to be "right" or to win. In fact, seeing the other viewpoint gives a much broader perspective on what is so. It enhances our life, rather than threatening it.

7. *Don't be afraid to use outside resources.* By outside resources, I mean Al-Anon, counselors, therapists, Adult Children of Alcoholics, church groups, ministers, and other groups or people who may be able to help you communicate or to get in touch with your higher power.

It may seem strange to mention outside resources when we're talking about intimacy *within* the family, but remember that in some ways the family is one of the most difficult places to achieve intimacy. The family is a survival-oriented unit. That is the way it was designed, and vestiges of this purpose remain. Survival issues will be raised and Robots will come into play. You need someone outside the family who can act as a support for everyone and help you remember that there is Spirit beyond the Robot.

The family needs to be connected to that higher power in order to move into intimacy. Some people say they've never seen evidence of a higher power, or it's certainly not available to them, or they can only experience it when they're alone. This is like the man who got lost near the North Pole and whose dog team took off and left him. He prayed to God to save him. Later someone asked him if God had answered his prayer and he said, "No, but an Eskimo came along and brought me in on his sled."

Outside resources are helpful if you don't feel you are coping effectively with your family, or if someone else in your family doesn't seem to be coping well. By "coping" I mean being flexible, being willing to see another's point of view even when you don't agree with it, but not being so flexible that you are completely wishy-washy.

Some people are afraid to suggest help for someone in their family, because they don't want to interfere. In an intimate relationship, you make your concerns known. That doesn't mean making known your judgments, analyses, or interpretations—just your concerns. I often hear people saying, "You're an alcoholic," or "You're passive-aggressive" rather than saying "I'm noticing that you used to have two martinis every night, and now you have six before dinner. That concerns me because I know that one of the early symptoms of alcoholism is a high tolerance. I would really like you, or us, to talk to someone about this." Share your experience. Talk about yourself and your reactions to the other person's behavior, rather than assigning labels and telling him what's "wrong" with him.

The other person may not be very happy with your suggestion. He may rant and rave, but at least you have made yourself known. He may *feel* judged even if you haven't judged him. The difference between being a "co" for someone and simply making yourself known is one of intention. If you tell him your concern with no other intention than being genuine, that's intimacy. If you tell him so that he will *change*, it's "co-ing." When people say, "Well, there's no point in saying anything. It isn't going to make any difference," they really mean, "He's not going to change anyway."

If you need to talk to someone in your family about getting help, do it. Don't let your Robot talk you out of it. When you have told the truth to another, you are free to go on to the next level of truth about yourself. If you hadn't said it, you would be stuck with worry and silent disapproval.

When people hear the words "professional help," "psychologist," and "support group," they often still think of mental illness, unbalanced personalities, California, or some aberration. Nowadays there are many kinds of groups and approaches that are not designed for the mentally ill, but are ways to understand yourself and the Spirit.

We Americans often take a "do it yourself" attitude toward things. We think it makes us less independent or less strong if we seek help. That attitude can render us immobile.

The first step to solving any problem is to admit that it exists, and the first step to finding our connection with our higher power is to admit that our Robots are powerless over certain situations. Don't let the Robot's pride keep you from getting support from someone who can keep you in touch with the higher power and help you through difficult times.

When you seek help from friends or professionals, look for people who will do more than get you in touch with how you got "that way" and what awful people your parents were. Seek out people who focus on you and what you can do about your life, not on what others have done to you. You can't change your childhood; what you can change are the decisions you made in childhood and are living by today. That is what is keeping you trapped, not your parents' behavior. The emphasis should be on what your Robot did with those behaviors, on the decisions it made and how you can undo them.

You may first have to explore what happened with your parents in order to let go of any blame you may be laying on yourself, but the point is to discover what you are going to do about it *now*. Even if your father molested you, you have a choice about how to regard that today. You can let it determine the rest of your life, or you can discover the decisions you made and get support in letting go of them.

No matter how intimate you are with your family and friends, you may still benefit from outside support. Seeking outside help doesn't mean you are weak, or can't handle your own problems, or are unbalanced. It just means that you are willing to accept support, and that connecting with your higher power and with others is more important to you than looking good.

Communication is the best tool we have in achieving intimacy. All of the barriers to intimate communication come from the Robot's need to defend itself and to be "right." Letting go of our desire to protect ourselves with the Robot is the key to intimate communication. The more we become aware of how the Robot operates and what it is likely to do, the easier it becomes to move beyond that into Spirit, which is our ultimate goal.

THINGS TO DO

Look in the yellow pages for a support system for yourself. List those you find.

Ask friends if they belong to any groups and how they feel about them.

CHAPTER FIVE

WHERE INTIMACY BREAKS DOWN

If intimacy is a natural state, why don't more people experience it? Expectations, fears, and trying to protect ourselves from being hurt—in short, the Robot—all stand in the way. These barriers aren't bad; they're just part of the human condition. Discovering what they are and letting them go so that we can experience our connection with other people, ourselves, and the Spirit is a lifelong, ever-adventurous process.

These are some of the barriers to intimacy:

1. *Expectations* of what intimacy is and of how other people should be in intimate relationships.

Our Robots have in their file cabinets many ideas, opinions, beliefs, and expectations about how relationships should be. If someone asked, "What is a good friend?" most of us would be able to rattle off a list of qualities we expected to find. If the question was, "What is a good husband?" or "What is a good wife?" we could answer with many "shoulds."

Some of our Robots' ideas are taken from society, television, what somebody told us, or what we saw. Our Robots have come up with other decisions all by themselves, or developed them in reaction to certain situations. In any case, they are completely unpredictable except for one thing: Their purpose is to make the Robot "right." Some people might think, for instance, that the ideal husband is one who makes a lot of money and never shows his face around the house, who is never underfoot causing trouble and just leaves his wife and children alone to spend his money. Others might think the ideal husband is one who stays home with the kids all day, does the laundry and the dishes, and has dinner on the table when his wife comes home from work. We may have different expectations, but expectations are a fact of life. We all have them.

Some of us have such clever Robots that we say, "I really don't have any expectations. It doesn't matter if he takes care of the kids or brings home the bacon." Rest assured, the expectations are there—somewhere. Maybe we expect him to do a certain kind of work. Maybe our expectations have to do with sex. Maybe they are about how he should treat us, or how he should treat our family. The expectation might be as subtle as, "I'm giving him the freedom to be and do what he wants; he should do the same for me." This poor guy isn't going to be able to ask anything of us; whatever he says will be wrong.

The Robot's expectations are usually based on decisions it has made about the family in which we grew up. The Robot wants to be either *like* that family or *different* from it. Occasionally, there is another family involved, one with whom we were close, but usually it is the birth family. The Robot simply takes a look around at our upbringing and thinks, "That was great and I want to duplicate it," "That was awful and I want to do just the opposite," or something in between.

(It's important to remember that what the Robot thinks has nothing whatsoever to do with the truth. Our siblings may each have a different view.)

The point is not to get rid of our expectations. We can't do that; they will be with us as long as we are human. But we can prevent those expectations from becoming barriers to intimacy. The first step is to recognize them for what they are—decisions the Robot made when we were very young, perhaps decades ago, based on what it *thought* it had to do to be "right" and to survive.

The next step is to become aware of their exact content. When we get upset in intimate relationships, it is often because our expectations are not being met.

It is important to distinguish the way we *expect* things to be from the way we *want* things to be. We might want one thing, but believe that it is impossible. We might think, "Well, I'd like to be intimate with my family, but they just aren't the kind of people who could do it," or "I'd love to have a good marriage, but with my family background it's probably impossible." Knowing how our expectations of what we can have differ from what we actually want can prevent those expectations from getting in the way.

As a child, I had contact with two families outside my own who were quite different. In the first family, there was no respite from the fighting. Everyone yelled at each other. My stomach started churning whenever I went into that house. The second family lived in a house that was sunny and yellow and bright. Their family was out of a storybook. I used to walk to school with the daughter, and each morning the mother would be in the kitchen cooking bacon and seeing everyone off with a sunny smile.

I decided that the mother's happy disposition was the reason things were so wonderful in this family. I also decided that screaming and yelling was enough to make people sick.

These decisions became barriers to intimacy for me. As I grew older it became clear that I am *not* a person of sunny disposition in the morning. Faking it never fooled my kids. I finally got smart, told the truth about myself, and turned breakfast and mornings over to my husband, who is alert and cheery at that time of day.

Because of my decision about the dangers of yelling, I found it very difficult to raise my voice to my children. Unfortunately, the few times I did it my daughters almost fainted from the fright. The energy and explosiveness of my occasional outbursts were far out of proportion to the event.

The problem was not whether or not to yell, but that my *fear* of yelling made it persist as an issue. Now that I'm no longer afraid of yelling, I find very little reason to do so. The girls haven't fainted in a long time.

Decisions or expectations about how certain kinds of people are can also limit intimacy. I know a lot of women who have the expectation that men will be uncommunicative. Consequently, their Robots don't allow communicative men into their lives. Moreover, many men may not communicate in the style to which these women are accustomed, but they do communicate in their own ways—if the women are willing to heed. If we can be open to the various ways that communication takes place and accept them for what they are, this expectation will lose its power.

Expectations lead to disappointment. An example of this is people who date and date, and never find anyone who is good enough. They are perpetually disappointed. If people don't measure up by the second date, that's it for them. Control is the issue here. Usually, these people are actually afraid that *they* won't measure up for some reason. By getting into relationships with people who don't measure up to *their* standards, they avoid that possibility. They would rather be the "disappointed" than the "disappointee."

I worked with a couple recently whose relationship nearly foundered on unmet expectations. Sue was uncomfortable in social situations, and expected that when she and Hal went to parties, he stay right by her side and take care of her. She was quiet and shy, and loved having a gregarious, outgoing person like Hal around her. She expected that if he really loved her, he would support her, pay attention to her, and not talk to other women—especially pretty ones.

But she also had the conflicting expectation that he would not *want* to stay with her. Out of low self-esteem, she thought that he would want to talk to all the other women.

And it happened that Hal was always going off to talk to pretty women.

As we talked, it became clear to her that, in very subtle ways, she had actually manipulated him into a position where he felt forced to leave her alone and talk to other people. Her Robot had to support her expectation and was willing to put her through a lot of pain in order to be "right."

On the way to a party, Sue would manage to somehow put Hal on the defensive. Usually, she pushed his "inadequacy" button by teasing him about having lost a lot of money at poker the night before, or mention something that hadn't turned out well for him at work. By the time they got to the party, Hal needed to escape from her. This pattern continued until they were finally able to sit down and tell the truth to one another.

Hal realized that he had been trying to hide this "loser" button from Sue, because he was afraid she would use it to hurt him. She had discovered the button anyway, but he didn't want to admit that. He even went so far as to say, "That wasn't really what she meant to do." She hadn't done it deliberately, but her Robot had ways of making sure it happened.

Of course, Hal's own expectations of himself were that he was a loser and that someone would find out about it. But on the other hand, he had an expectation that Sue wouldn't use it against him, so she deserved to be punished if she did. Their crosscutting expectations were going up, down, around, and through. Once they were brought out into the open, however, this couple had the determination to deal with them.

They agreed to voice their expectations as simply expectations. That left the door open for communication.

So when Sue voiced her expectation that Hal stay by her side at a party, Hal no longer experienced it as a demand. Sue no longer thought of it as the thing a loving husband should do, and they could talk about their choices in the matter.

As it turned out, Hal was far more willing to stay with Sue some of the time now that he no longer felt chastised for not doing so, and Sue felt much less need to have him around now that she knew his absence didn't mean he didn't love her.

Parents and children have many expectations of one another. As parents, we want our children to feel good about themselves, to express themselves, and to bring forth their greatest abilities and talents. Sometimes, however, we insist that they do it in a way that is acceptable to us. We don't like it if their way seems "inappropriate" or off the wall, and sometimes we fight them on it. This forces them either to avoid making themselves known to us or to rebel against us, and that is not what anyone wants.

We have to remember that our kids are not amorphous lumps of clay, placed on earth for us to mold. They are human beings with their own growth processes and their own choices to make. That doesn't mean we have no control over them and have to let them do whatever they want, but we do need to listen to them and respond to them if we want our relationships with them to be intimate. We must be especially careful to root out our hidden expectations for them.

My client Ray feels that his own ambitions of becoming a major-league baseball player had been squashed by his father, who insisted that he go to law school. Ray became a successful attorney, but now is having difficulties in his relationship with his own son, who is nine. Ray says, "I don't want to do to him what my father did to me." He wants his son to have the chance to play ball professionally, coaches him every weekend, and goes to all the Little League games. His son is actually something of a bookworm. He's interested in music, and not particularly athletic. In trying to avoid doing what his father had done, Ray is doing exactly the same thing.

Parents aren't the only people with expectations and Robots. Children try to enforce their expectations with as much sophistication and subtlety as their parents. What children are after with their parents is *power*.

Most children—and many adults—believe that the way to get power is to get control over other people. This is the Robot's way of being in control. Ultimately, of course, the only true control is our connection with our higher power. But growing up is about finding out "who we are not," and part of that is discovering that getting control over other people is not the way to find fulfillment or satisfaction.

To a child, getting control of his environment means getting control of his parents. They are the people he wants to please. They are his first chance to make a contribution, to bring joy, and to love. When he doesn't feel like he is bringing joy and making a contribution—and no matter how wonderful the child, or the parents, this is not always going to be the case—he fights even harder for control. It is in these moments that facade-building begins: fooling people to make them think that he is lovable, even when he doesn't believe it himself.

We all want to bring joy into one another's lives. We all want to love and be loved. The expectations we have about one another are just defenses to protect us from *not* having that experience of love and sharing. Ironically, they can be the very things that prevent it.

2. *Fear of loss* is another barrier to intimacy. When I begin to reveal myself to someone I love, it is indeed possible that one or both of us may want to leave the relationship, because the things we find out about ourselves and one another may be too uncomfortable. If real intimacy is important to me, those are risks I have to take.

Mark is a man in his fifties with four grown children. A year after his wife died, he discovered that he was gay and began living with a man he loved. It took him a while to come to terms with his own sexuality, and even then he had to decide whether or not to tell his children. He knew he risked losing their support, and maybe even their love, but on the other hand he didn't want to hide this important part of his life from them. He loved them very much and wanted to be in their lives, but he also wanted them to know who he was.

One daughter accepted the situation readily. She was a little surprised, and even somewhat amused, but she was delighted that he was happy and glad he had someone to love. The other daughter accepted the situation somewhat less enthusiastically. She was glad he was living the way he wanted to live, and that he had felt good enough about their relationship to tell her, but she didn't want her children to know. Mark's sons weren't at all happy about their father's revelation. It took one son six months to accept Mark's sexuality, and the other one never did.

These reactions were painful for Mark. He lost one of his sons, and he doesn't see his other son and the reluctant daughter as much as he once had. All of the relationships are changed in some way.

On one level, Mark's relationships with three of his children are now more limited. On another level, they are richer. Even the son who wants nothing to do with Mark knows more about him than he ever did, and Mark knows more about him. The other son and reluctant daughter have seen completely new dimensions in their father—not just his homosexuality, but his willingness to reveal himself in this way. They in turn have had a chance to see how they react to change, to homosexuality, and to someone they love risking a lot for intimacy with them.

It's almost impossible to predict what will happen when you take the risk for intimacy. People's reactions may be better than you think they will be, or they may be worse. The one thing you do know is that there will be change. The only reason to take that risk is love and the fuller expression of love that intimacy brings forth. The people to whom we reveal ourselves know that on some level, no matter what their reactions. They may not be able to accept it, but they know they've been given a gift.

3. *Communicating from the Robot rather than Spirit* puts a tremendous strain on intimate relationships, for the Robot's communication is designed specifically to protect us from being known and knowing others. Messages are neither sent nor received with clarity or accuracy.

Walter Adams has an image of what it means to be a good father and a good provider. He brings home the money, and in return he feels that he should have the final word in family matters. He never says it in so many words, he doesn't think it is a particularly enlightened point of view, and he may not even be aware that he has it, but when push comes to shove, everybody knows that Daddy holds the purse strings.

His wife, Cathy, thinks of herself as liberated. She makes sure she has her say and is allowed to do what she wants, but in the end she believes she is subservient to her husband and knows she can only be independent so far. After all, he is the breadwinner and she has to watch her step. She might insist on going to the beach rather than the park for the picnic, but Walter is the one who decides whether or not the family is going on the picnic in the first place.

When Cathy announced that she wanted to get a job and then started working as a receptionist in a law office, Walter didn't actually come out and say how upset he was, because that would have made him look bad, but he made snide remarks about her work and how it cost as much to pay the cleaning lady as she made. He would look disgruntled and annoyed when dinner wasn't on the table at 6:30, and refuse to help around the house. He'd never done it before; why should he do it now? The message behind his communication was that Cathy might work as many hours as he did, but she didn't bring home as much money so she wasn't worth as much.

Cathy's Robot was making subtle statements, too. She sensed Walter's resentment and lack of cooperation, and made it her business to prove how important her job was. She volunteered for extra work and brought it home with her. That left her even less time to do the things that she had always done for the family.

Cathy and Walter were trying to tell one another that they felt threatened as the family homeostasis was upset, that they needed attention and wanted to be reassured of one another's love. Unfortunately, only the Robots were communicating and so the messages weren't getting through.

The Robot will never go away. We can't get rid of it, but we can begin to recognize it. That gives us power over it. We can either nip its communications in the bud or acknowledge to other people that it's just our Robot.

Walter might have noticed that he felt slighted when Cathy wasn't there with dinner when he came home, and seen that he wasn't as liberated and enlightened as he had thought. He might have said, "Gee, I didn't realize I was going to have this kind of reaction. You don't have to change anything, but sometimes if I'm acting a little sulky it's because there's a part of me that feels very threatened by your being out there in the world. There's also a part of me that doesn't see why you're doing this, because it doesn't seem to be good for the family, and it's costing us at least as much money as it's bringing in. On the other hand, I realize there is a part of you that really needs to do it."

Cathy might have made herself known by saying something like, "This is a little harder than I thought it would be. I'm feeling defensive, and want to justify having a job. I resent it when I come home and the house is a mess, because it seems like no one is doing anything to help. In fact, sometimes it seems like everyone is working hard to make this harder for me and punish me for wanting to get out there and express myself. It's not really that I expect everyone to change to accommodate me, but it's important for me to let you know what I'm thinking about myself and how defensive I'm getting."

When the other person isn't revealing what we want, the Robot is inclined to distort his meaning and to interpret his communication according to the Robot's needs.

Marge didn't think her husband, Gerry, was at all interested in her work, so it became very important to her that
he come to the office Christmas party and meet all her col-
leagues. This would somehow prove to her that he was interested, or else convince him he ought to be interested.
Gerry had reluctantly promised to come, but the day of the
party he started having chest pains and shooting pains down
his left arm. He was frightened and went to the doctor instead
of the Christmas party.

Marge thought he had fabricated the whole thing so he
wouldn't have to go to her party, but six weeks later he had
a heart attack.

The office party obviously wasn't the real reason Gerry
had his heart attack, but Marge had missed some opportunities. She might have simply accepted that Gerry wasn't interested in her work and found someone else to take to the
office party. She might have told Gerry she was disappointed
that she didn't think he cared about her work, but then gone
ahead and found other ways to connect with him.

Children's communication can range from open and
honest to covert and manipulative, especially in their teens.
Teenagers are exploring all sorts of styles of communicating.
Their Robots are trying to find out how to get control, to
discover what responses it gets to what behaviors. Teens are
having their first experiences of power, so it may be expecting
too much for them to sit down immediately and tell the truth
about how they're feeling, even if they are aware of it, which
often they are not.

Parents have to be prepared for their children to think
they are wrong no matter what they do, and even be willing
simply to say, "It seems that no matter what I do, it's wrong."

Robots like to gang up on people. If three members of
the family are communicating and the fourth is not, the Robots want to get together and figure out what they can do to
"fix Joey." If you do discuss a family problem without one
of the people present, it's important to keep the discussion
in the first person: "What I'm noticing about *myself* in this

process is . . ." Maybe Joey needs to know exactly where the boundaries are, and everyone must see clearly how they are supporting Joey in keeping within those boundaries—or not.

Maybe Joey's father is tough, and his mother is lenient. Maybe his sister looks so good compared to him that she provokes his bad behavior. While they are not causing Joey's problems, they may be participating in them. It's a good idea to sit down and talk about that participation. The mother might say, "I see myself giving in to Joey when I shouldn't." The father might say, "I don't want to bother with him so I just send him to his room or ground him." The sister might say, "I see myself deliberately provoking him when you're around so he'll start yelling at me and you'll get mad at him."

We've been talking about family situations, but the same dynamics are likely to occur in any relationship. The key is to recognize when the Robot takes over the communication, and acknowledge it.

4. *Holding on to the past* is another barrier to intimacy. The Robot is not forgiving. Besides holding tightly to old resentments, it also enjoys using old behaviors in new relationships. Intimacy is about freeing ourselves of these Robot-like behaviors and resentments.

It is hard to escape the past, but we don't have to let it determine our future. Our biological families present us with the chance to learn certain lessons. If there is an alcoholic in our family, perhaps we need to learn something about alcoholism or compassion. If we are born into a family that demanded high achievement, perhaps we need to learn that we can't earn love.

We can't escape the lessons by escaping the people in our biological families. Those same lessons will come up again with different people. Only by learning them can we move forward. As long as we are alive, there will be more lessons to learn, and so we will always be dealing with our past on some level. We can ease that process, however, by recognizing and eliminating some of the Robot's past resentments and behaviors. We don't have to be slaves to the past, especially if we learn the old lessons and move on to new ones.

Bill and Sue had two children, Alice and Tim. Instead of relating to Bill, Alice, and Tim as husband, daughter, and son, Sue related to them as she had related to her three siblings. She had been the Perfect Child in her own family, so made Bill the Rebel (which worked out very well, because he was an alcoholic and was always doing something wrong), Tim the Loner, and Alice the Charmer. Once again, she was the "little mother" to three children, just as she had been when she was young. Once more, she was the responsible one, the one who took care of everybody. But this left Sue without a helpmate. There was no one to support her in raising these three children.

Tim and Alice saw Sue as the "mean" parent, the disciplinarian, the one who made life difficult for everybody. They also saw that their father was really more like a brother than a father, and joined with him in a conspiracy against Sue. This was exactly what had happened in Sue's biological family: Her three siblings had joined together to discredit the Perfect Child.

Sue had hoped that when she got out on her own, married, and had her own family, she would have people who really appreciated her and loved her, people who wouldn't gang up on her. Instead, she had unconsciously re-created exactly the same situation in which she grew up. She felt betrayed, let down, disappointed, and unappreciated—exactly the things she had felt while growing up.

Without knowing it, Sue had let her Robot take over. The Robot's decision was that people ganged up on her, and it had gone to great lengths in order to be "right."

Through Al-Anon, an organization for the family and friends of alcoholics, Sue began to see what she had done. She found ways to let go of the past and her need to be "right." She started to make herself known to her family as a human being, not as a Perfect Child, and that in turn released them from the rigidity of their roles.

Perry and Barbara also had to deal with roles left over from their original families. They loved one another, but knew that something was missing in their communication. Barbara had been the Charmer in her own family, the cute little one whom everyone adored. She had an older sister who was the Perfect Child, and another sister who was the Rebel. Barbara had decided she didn't want anything to do with either of those roles, particularly the Rebel role, because that sister got into a staggering amount of trouble.

Perry had been a Loner. He, too, had a Rebel sibling, a brother who caused a lot of problems in the family, and he didn't want Rebels around him any more than Barbara did.

Barbara being a Charmer and Perry being a Loner worked out very well. She was witty, charming, and adorable, which complemented his tendency to withdraw, do his own thing, and not relate to people much. It was a perfect match, except for one thing. Because Perry and Barbara had both avoided conflict as children, neither of them had ever learned to fight. In fact, neither of them could stand fighting, because it reminded them of their Rebel siblings.

When they were dating, there hadn't been much trouble. Barbara would charm Perry out of his shell, and he would create a nice, quiet environment that she learned to enjoy. But after they got married, things changed. Perry would go off by himself for hours, and no amount of cuteness or charm would bring him out. Barbara began to get anxious, annoyed, and irritable. She couldn't understand why he wasn't responding to her, and blamed him because her charm wasn't working. Her temper began to flare. Perry couldn't stand her screaming at him and lashed back at her. They both wound up doing the thing they hated most—yelling and fighting—and blamed the other for causing so much trouble.

They began to see one another as the Rebel siblings they had always resisted. They had never liked Rebel behavior in their siblings, and they didn't like it in each other. Worse, they were beginning to see this kind of behavior in *themselves*, and they liked that even less. In one another's presence, they were becoming exactly like those argumentative, difficult people they had grown up with. The few times they recognized this behavior in themselves, they blamed the other for it, but mostly they only saw it in one another.

Through counseling, they began to see what was happening and to look at their own behaviors. Once they started to understand the dynamic, they could talk about it. They realized how the old patterns were triggered, and that there was something available to them beyond their Robots. They had to make room for the upsets, of course—it's only human—but they also saw that they could move beyond their Robots' reactions and start communicating as Perry and Barbara, not as the Rebel siblings.

Jim Stanton had another way of using the past. He and his wife, Peggy, had been married for thirty years. Things went fairly smoothly until Peggy started to bring up things she didn't like about their marriage, as well as those she did. Jim couldn't stand to hear anything negative about their relationship, and every time Peggy said something he received as criticism, his Robot brought out the heavy defenses.

The ammunition his Robot used was the one night Peggy had spent with another man, years before they were married. He was the only other man Peggy had ever slept with, but Jim just wouldn't let her forget it. Whenever he felt out of control of their arguments, he would drag out this incident and say, "I'll never be able to trust you. And anyway, what right do you have to criticize me after what you did?"

That was the end of the conversation, because Peggy had no defense. She had done it, and couldn't say she hadn't. Of course, years earlier she had thrown the same incident in his face when she was angry. He had come home very late and she had said, "Well, you've probably been out with someone. I'm sure you have, but you're not the only one who's done that kind of thing." The one night Peggy had spent with the other man became a hand grenade that they threw back and forth at one another anytime they needed a weapon.

I made them sign an agreement never to bring up the event in an argument. This proved to be almost impossible for them. I watched them start to bring it up and stop, start to bring it up and stop. Jim suddenly had a revealing memory. As a child, a little boy he thought was his best friend had criticized him severely, and that incident ended the friendship. Jim's Robot had decided that the other little boy had left him, and that when people criticize you, they are about to desert you. His fear was that if Peggy criticized him, she would leave.

Jim later realized that, in fact, the little friend hadn't deserted him. He had deserted the friend, and his greater fear was not that Peggy would leave, but that *he* would leave. Every time he brought up this incident, he did, in effect, go away, because there was nowhere for the conversation to go after that. He was doing to Peggy what he had done to his friend, out of fear that she would do to him what he *thought* his friend had done to *him*. Once he saw that, it was much easier to give up using that one incident to be "right."

5. *Resentments* are hurts that the Robot brings up over and over again and uses to make other people "wrong." Resentments have a recurring, stonewalling quality about them. The Robot ruminates on past resentments, building up huge cases against other people. Moving beyond resentments means being willing to look just as "bad" as the people we resent.

Bobbie's older sister had been very much the Perfect Child, the hero of the family. When they were growing up, Bobbie had always admired her, respected her, and looked up to her, but at times she had also resented all the attention and accolades this sister had received. Without being aware of it, Bobbie had spent a good part of her life trying to compete with her sister. When she realized she couldn't really compete on the sister's own turf, Bobbie went out and found some new territory.

Her sister had always been inclined to be somewhat materialistic. She was interested in Guccis, Vuittons, designer clothes, and always surrounded herself with nice things. Bobbie had a natural inclination toward the esoteric and the spiritual. She didn't realize that her Robot grasped this quality and used it to be "right." Now Bobbie had a reason for the difficulties in their relationship: The sister wasn't enlightened. Bobbie could now resent her sister, because she wasn't on the same "plane of existence" as Bobbie, and was more interested in shopping than in meditating.

In my talks with Bobbie, another element of the story emerged. When their father died years earlier, the two sisters had gone over to his house to divide up his things. Bobbie's sister had been living in the same community with their father and had spent more time with him in recent years, but it was assumed that they would divide his things equally. When they got to the house, Bobbie realized that some of his things were gone, but she didn't think much about it. A few months later, she visited her sister and saw all that had been missing.

Bobbie's resentment had crystallized, not because she decided her sister was unenlightened, but because the sister had taken these things from their father's house. Bobbie couldn't bring it up, however, because then she would have looked just as materialistic as the sister. Over the years, this resentment had grown to the point that they rarely even saw one another.

Bobbie's Robot knew that in order to make herself known, she would have to admit her interest in material things. In fact, she was going to have to look just as "wrong" as she had made her sister all these years. Bobbie had to recognize that we all have human qualities and that we're not going to die if other people find out about them or even use them against us. Revealing ourselves, even when it is painful, is the only way to find intimacy. Bobbie found that it was actually a small price to pay. In return she got an intimate relationship with her sister that lasted the rest of their lives, as well as some of the furniture that had been in her father's house.

6. *Trying to change others* is not only a barrier to intimacy, it is absolutely futile. So many of life's problems seem to be the other guy's fault. We spend a lot of time talking with our friends about how if only Joe would change, if only he'd pick up his clothes, or stop drinking, or get a better job, then things would be better for us. If only Jane would keep the house nicer, or stop being catty, or be better with the children . . .

Every minute we spend in such futile speculation is a minute spent not discovering the truth about ourselves and what we can do about the situation to make it work for us. It keeps the problem frozen, rather than helping us release it. It keeps us from having to look at uncomfortable things about ourselves, but doesn't create any solutions. Joe may never learn to pick up his socks, but that doesn't have to make my life miserable. I have choices. If I don't want to pick them up every day, I can simply tell him that every time I have to pick up his socks, I'm going to put them in the wastebasket instead of his drawer.

Some people realize that they can't change other people, but accept this realization with a martyred resignation. They say, "That's just the way they are and I can't do anything about it." This makes them victims. They refuse to develop new avenues and solutions so that Joe's problems don't become theirs. Joe may never get a better job, but they can go out and get one to increase the family income. He may not stop drinking, but they have a choice about whether or not to stay with him.

People are often afraid that the only two alternatives are (1) keep nagging the person until he changes, or (2) give up and become a victim. We may have to resign ourselves to the fact that the other person will never change, but the next step is to move into action. That's uncomfortable, because the one we have to act on is ourselves. We have to find out what it is about the other person's behavior that triggers us, and what we can do to make the situation work for us *without* the other person changing.

A lot of people are willing to reveal themselves, but their hidden expectation is that when they do, the other person will change. They say, "When you don't put the cap on the toothpaste, it makes me nuts." The next morning, they are appalled to find the cap still off! Well, it just doesn't work that way. The purpose of making ourselves known is to reveal ourselves, not to change the other person.

The classic example of trying to get others to change by revealing oneself is "intervention" with an alcoholic. This is a technique in which the family members and friends of the alcoholic sit down with him and tell him how they feel when he behaves in certain ways. The point of intervention is for the people around the alcoholic to take charge of their own lives, stop being victimized by him, and make known to him what they intend to do.

In some cases, however, people do this with the expectation that the alcoholic will change, that he will stop drinking. In fact, they do it with the intention of forcing the alcoholic to change and are furious with him if he doesn't. That isn't intervention; it's blackmail.

Trying to change someone works only when the person being changed wants to be a victim. If this is the case, look out. Sooner or later, he will call in the debt you "owe" him because he changed for you, and it's likely to be very expensive.

7. *You can't ever get enough of what you don't want.* We've all known people who went after money and possessions, thinking these things would make them happy, and then found out that they didn't. When it comes to material things, it's almost a cliché that you can't have enough of what you realize later you don't really want. But it's also true when it comes to people.

Loving, intimate relationships can bring happiness, but the happiness doesn't come from the other person. It comes from what you discover and learn to love about yourself in the relationship with the other person, and from the joy of sharing that process and watching the other person find happiness in himself as well.

People often enter into a relationship thinking it will bring them self-esteem, prestige, security, excitement, or just plain "settling in" so that they don't have to be concerned anymore with the constant search for relationships. But somehow things don't work out, and then they are disappointed. Usually, they begin the search again. They look for a "better person," but they are never really satisfied. That is because the void we ultimately want to fill is not filled by another person, however he may relate to us.

All any of us really wants in life is to love, to be intimate, and to be connected with our higher power. Nothing else will satisfy us. We will keep looking until we find those things.

The things we think we *should* want, the things we've been taught to want, are not necessarily what we *do* want. Those things might bring us status or prestige, but they will never bring us satisfaction or self-worth.

The Robot looks to other people to complete us or make us whole. Not only is the other person to blame if we're not happy, but it distracts us from the one thing that *will* make us feel whole—the Spirit. We come down to a choice between being "right" or having what we truly want. If you constantly feel disappointed or let down in relationships, this might be something to consider.

My client Marsha felt that her mother always let her down, never came through for her, and gave her no support. After several sessions in which she thoroughly lambasted her mother, I had to talk to her about her unpaid bill. She said,

"Oh, I gave it to my mother because she's going to take care of this." Marsha was an adult with her own career. She could easily have paid her own bill, but her mother wanted to pay it. Nonetheless, Marsha refused to see that her mother was demonstrating in the best way she knew that she loved and supported her daughter. Marsha just couldn't receive the message, because she had been looking to her mother for another kind of support.

Marsha had a hard time letting go of the idea that she would feel worthwhile if only her mother would behave in certain ways. Ultimately, she had to realize that only she, and her connection with the higher power, could give her that self-esteem.

Many parents feel that their children are letting them down if they don't get good grades, behave nicely, excel at sports, get good jobs, or marry the right people. Kids feel their parents are letting them down if they aren't there for them constantly, fixing things for them, and approving of everything they do. Naturally, this puts impossible burdens on everyone, and no one gets what he or she wants.

This dynamic is subtle and complex. If I expect you to make me feel a certain way, then you are responsible for how I feel. If that's the case, then on some level, I believe that I'm responsible for how *you* feel. I have to do my best to be the way I think you want me to be so that I don't let you down and make you feel bad. I can't do that, of course, but I try very hard. And every time you accuse me of *not* doing that, I flare up and get furious because I'm trying so hard and you don't appreciate it. It's definitely a no-win situation.

8. *Needing to be needed* is a variation on this theme. It's true that none of us really needs to be in relationships in order to survive, but people who are always saying, "I don't need anybody," are usually the very people who, deep down, feel that they *do* need someone. They need someone who needs *them*. They feel they have to be needed in order to survive.

Claire was a woman whose survival was tied up in needing to be needed, not just by her children but by her husband. In the long run, her children found this debilitating. She did everything for them. They didn't have to work around the house, get summer jobs, or look after their basic daily needs. When they became adults and went out into the world, they were surprised that no one was doing these things for them. They found it pretty upsetting to have to make a living and learn to cope with all the discomforts from which their mother had protected them.

The dynamic was similar with Claire's husband, Will. Not only did she do everything for him, but she was so dependent on his needing her that she could never reveal anything about herself that might upset him. Nor could she hear anything from him that indicated in any way that he might leave, or that he was even slightly dissatisfied. In this situation, no one could tell the truth about anything. Will sensed that he had better not criticize Claire, and became more and more closed off from her. He found someone else he could talk to, though: his secretary.

The kids loved having everything done for them— for a while. But they had no respect or appreciation for Claire and ultimately had little respect for themselves for treating her like the hired help. This put tremendous pressure on the relationship and kept them from being truly intimate.

People who need to be needed are often desperate to have a relationship. Their identity depends on being part of a couple with someone—anyone. They are often *not* in relationships, of course, because nothing drives people away faster than being needed for someone else's survival. It's hard to be exposed to desperation, whether in a friendship or a romantic relationship, for underneath it is anger—the anger of powerlessness that comes out of need.

When we need to be needed, we can't be intimate, because we don't dare tell the truth. The other person might leave. We don't want to hear the truth from them, either, because they might say something that threatens the relationship. We forget that the higher power is within ourselves, and that it is the only thing we really need or that anyone else really needs.

9. *The idea that love is something we have to earn* may be the most powerful barrier to intimacy, and it is utterly false. Love already exists, for all of us. We have barriers to experiencing that love, but they are not insurmountable. We come to experience love by letting go of those barriers, not by earning it. In fact, there is absolutely nothing we can do to earn love, as people who have spent a lifetime trying will attest.

One major misconception held by many is that love is a *feeling*. Love is simply not a feeling; it is a state in which we want people, including ourselves, to fulfill their own potential and connect with their higher power. We can experience this state of being at will.

Thus, we can love people without necessarily having a feeling of "love" toward them. I've heard people say, "How can I love my father, after what he said and did?" Yet, in truth, they still want the best for their fathers and would like to experience loving them. It's often this desire to feel love for someone that gets us into trouble. We think, "If only he would change this or that, I could love him." We get angry that certain things about him keep us from loving him, and we blame him for those things. In the process of trying to get him to change and causing him to resist us, we set up a struggle and move even further away from feeling love.

We get the idea that love has to be earned because there are times when we force other people to earn *our* love. This never works, of course, because what people really love about us is ourselves. Anything we add to or subtract from that becomes a barrier.

The things we do to earn love are usually the very things that make us unlovable, because they are denials of our true natures and our individual expressions. By trying to change ourselves to earn love, we camouflage our true natures and in the process make it harder for people to see what it is they truly love about us.

My friend Sally had trouble experiencing love for her father because he was such a loudmouth. He had probably developed that characteristic as a child, when it was the only way he could get attention from his family. Most of our be- haviors are developed as young children for just that purpose—to get love, or at least attention, which of course is the booby prize. The result is that a lot of these behaviors are obnoxious. The Robot carries them into later life because they worked the first time. They still get attention, but it's apt to be negative.

Believing that love has to be earned also prevents us from having the experience of loving. Very few people will mea- sure up to our standards, and so we don't allow ourselves to experience loving them.

Ideas about how people have to be in order for us to love them are generated by a natural desire to protect ourselves from being hurt. If I don't make people earn my love, I might love too indiscriminately. If the person I love turns out to be a cocaine addict, or a womanizer, I'll be hurt.

But if I don't open myself up to the pain, I will never experience the love. I have to be able to trust myself to deal with the situation, including the possible loss. It's actually possible for us to love everyone on earth. All we have to do is let go of the idea that others have to earn our love, and we have to earn theirs.

10. *The idea that others are doing less than they are capable of doing* is a very common barrier to intimacy. It's hard to believe that people are doing their best when they keep mak- ing mistakes and doing things that hurt us, but we are all human beings with human frailties. The fact is, we're doing the best we can with the information and capabilities we have at any given moment.

Of someone who is chronically late, we think, "He could be on time if he wanted to be. He's just thoughtless and inconsiderate." But why is that person always late, and how long has he been doing that? Chances are, he's been doing it all his life, and his Robot probably has a very good reason. Maybe it was the only way he could get attention when he was young. Maybe he had a parent or sibling who was compulsively on time, and he is rebelling against a behavior that made him look bad. It doesn't matter what the reason is. The point is, you don't have to be victimized by his behavior and you don't have to blame him for it.

In a nonintimate relationship, you might not say anything to such a person out of politeness. If you are in an intimate relationship, however, you have to deal with the problem. Examine how you feel when he is late and what you want to do about it, given the fact that he is probably not going to change. Without blame, you can say, "Look, you've been late thirteen times this week, and the next time you're late, I'm not going to wait for you."

Children are prime examples of people doing the best they can, even when it doesn't look that way. When small children are stubborn or throw tantrums, they are usually just trying to communicate their displeasure, get attention, or define themselves in some way. Teenagers are constantly trying out new behaviors in an attempt to find out who they are and what works for them.

You don't have to sit still for everything they do, but it helps to understand that they really are trying their best. You can make your feelings known to them and set limits for them without accusing them of deliberately trying to make you miserable.

Think of a time when you weren't trying to do your best. There may be times when you *didn't* do your best, but it may be hard to remember a time when you weren't at least trying.

We're human. We get tired, irritable, angry, and resistant. We may not meet every situation the way we would like to, but we are always doing the best we can under the circumstances.

11. *The idea that people are not communicating when in fact they are* is insidious. Everything communicates all the time: silence, facial expression and body posture, slamming a door, a touch or the lack of a touch. The communication may not be direct or clear, but it is there if you look for it.

Olivia began to think that Paul didn't love her, because he never came home for dinner. He worked late every night and even went to the office on weekends. She began to think he was working so much just to avoid her. Paul believed that the way you told someone you loved her was to be a good provider. The harder you worked, the more you loved her. Olivia never actually told him how she felt, and he missed the signals she was putting out by being quiet and withdrawn. If they had been a little more sensitive to one another, and let go of their expectation of what communication looked like, they might have reconnected sooner.

If you don't understand what certain behaviors mean, it's a good idea to ask. Paul might have asked Olivia why she was so quiet and encouraged her to tell him what was wrong. She might have asked him why he was working so hard and if he was trying to avoid her.

Sometimes communications are just "in the air." I know that my two daughters love me to pieces, but you might not pick up on that if you were to have dinner at our house, because they tease me mercilessly. They make fun of me, laugh at me, and kid me about everything. It's very good for me, because not many people in my life do that. They constantly bring me down to earth and remind me that I'm laughable, funny, peculiar, weird—and lovable.

The Robot is at the root of every barrier to intimacy. Recognize what it is doing, gently put it aside, and move into Spirit. You may feel vulnerable at first, because some of these barriers have been in place a long time, but the discomfort is a small price to pay for the joy of being able to reveal yourself to others, let them reveal themselves to you, and share their love.

QUESTIONS TO ASK YOURSELF AND THINGS TO DO

What are your expectations of your family? List them.

What are you afraid of losing if you become intimate with your family. List these things.

What rationalizations and justifications and excuses do you have for avoiding intimacy with your family? List.

What past hurts and injustices are you holding on to in order to avoid intimacy with your family?

What resentments are keeping you from being intimate with your family?

Who in your family are you still hoping will change?

What are you using as substitutes for intimacy?

Who in your family needs you more than you need them?

Whose love are you still trying, or hoping, to earn?

Who is still trying to earn your love?

Who do you believe could do or could have done better in their relationship with you?

Who has been communicating with you all along, only you just weren't aware of it?

Who just doesn't "measure up"?

CHAPTER SIX

INTIMACY IN YOUR BIOLOGICAL FAMILY

Now that people are becoming more aware of family dynamics and the role they play in shaping our behavior, many seem dissatisfied with their biological family. We have discovered the "dysfunctional family," and now everybody seems to have had one. We're inclined to blame our families for our problems or limitations. The idea of changing those family dynamics to allow for intimacy seems overwhelming.

Yet these are the people with whom we live (or lived) and whom we are most apt to love. Whether we interpret biological family to mean the family into which you were born or the family that you became when you got married and had children, it seems like a good place to begin intimacy. It may turn out not to be possible to create intimacy in your biological family, but it's an option that is worth exploring—especially since whatever problems exist will probably emerge again in whatever kind of family you ultimately create for yourself.

Some people look at their biological families and just roll their eyes. Their father was a tough guy who never showed

his feelings and bossed everyone around. Their mother was
a martyr who expressed her own frustrations by criticizing
everybody else. The siblings were either smug perfectionists
or such a mess that there was danger of contamination. The
situation was so far from intimacy that it's difficult even to
imagine these people sitting down and revealing themselves
to one another. The dynamic has been in place for so long
—perhaps ten, twenty, forty, or sixty years—that the thought
of introducing intimacy is staggering.

Still, it takes only one person to change the dynamics, to
alter the homeostasis. When one person shifts, everyone has
to shift. It's possible that no one in the family has ever considered the option of intimacy in the way we've defined it.
It's also possible that everyone would find it very appealing,
but no one wants to be the first to rock the boat. The fact
that you are reading this book suggests that if anyone is going
to introduce intimacy, it's going to be you.

When we think of family, we tend to think in terms of
black and white. At first, there is a tendency to think that we
either have to create this high level of intimacy in our family
in, say, two weeks, or else we just need to chuck the whole
thing and find some new people to be our family. This is not
the case at all. We have many options.

It may be possible to create intimacy with some members
of your family and not with others. You may think you hate
your family because every time you go to a family dinner,
you are miserable. If you look again, you may find that it's
really just one sibling, perhaps sister Lynnie, who is sitting
across the table making you nuts. Maybe everyone is waiting
on her hand and foot, and she's just sitting there sulking. If
that's the case, and if you either don't think there is much
chance of intimacy with her or don't even want to attempt
it, you may find ways of relating to the rest of the family that
don't necessarily include her.

Your mother might say, "I don't know what's the matter
with you. You're not interested in having Lynnie over and

she needs our help and our concern." Maybe you can't invite all the rest of the family over and exclude Lynnie, but you can go out to lunch with your mother or have your brother and his wife over for dinner without including her. And you don't have to wait until Christmas, Thanksgiving, Easter, or Groundhog Day to do it. These are going to be new relationships, and you may want to start creating new forms for them.

Remember, your biological family is not your last chance for intimacy. If you start making yourself known to your family, and you just can't stand what's coming back to you, there are many other people to choose from. Among them you can probably find three, four, or five with whom you can create a new family. Don't put too much pressure on yourself to change everything in your family, right away, but do explore the possibilities.

The first step to creating intimacy in your biological family is to make a choice about whether that is really something you want to do.

Choosing Your Biological Family

Before you can commit to creating intimacy in your biological family, you have to choose to do so. These exercises are designed to help you make that choice:

1. *Examine your expectations.* What are your pictures of how a family should be and how you should feel in a family? Are you throwing your family over because they are not the Waltons or the Brady Bunch? Does everyone have to love and respect one another all the time, communicate perfectly from their Spirit, and act in ways that are acceptable to you?

What are your expectations of intimacy? Does it mean sitting in front of the fire together telling deep, dark secrets?

Do you need for family members to approve of you? Do you want just the "good" parts, without all the discomfort? Do you mind "looking bad" in front of them?

There may be things you absolutely require in a family, but we all have some expectations that aren't going to be realized in *any* family. It's important to see what those expectations are, and let go of them.

2. *Accept that this is how it is in your family and that this is probably how it's going to be.* Look at what your family dynamics actually are, rather than at what your pictures of them have been or what you think they *could* be. You may be holding a mental picture of your family that was true when you were a child, but that has shifted over the years.

Or you may be seeing your family in terms of "if only." If only Bob would stop drinking . . . if only Mother would relax or find a job . . . if only Dad would stop thinking about work all the time . . . if only Addie developed some compassion . . . *then* I could be intimate with them.

You have to make your choice for intimacy based on how it is right now, this minute. Things may change, but you can't count on that, and if they do change, they may not change in the directions that you expect or that you want. Assume that this is it, that nothing is going to change, and make your choice based on that.

If your mother and father don't speak to one another, that may not change just because you start making yourself known to them. If your husband comes home from work, pours himself a drink, and flops in front of the television until bedtime, he may continue doing that for the rest of his life. Your children may bicker until they are ninety.

You might even want to write down some facts about your family to make it very clear how things are. You may come up with things like:

"Every time I see my brother, he teases me about my weight."

"My mother doesn't approve of my selling lingerie, and probably never will."

"My father is never going to come out and say he loves me."

Look at your family as if for the first time, and recognize that this is how it is.

3. *Given that this is how it is, what can you do to fulfill your own needs?* You don't have to approve of your family's behaviors in order to live with them and have your own needs fulfilled. If your husband spends every night in front of television, maybe you can use that time to call up your girlfriends and chat, or go to the movies with your sister. Maybe you want to join a church group or a peace organization. You don't have to sit there watching him watch television. If he plays golf all day Saturday and Sunday, you might want to develop an interest of your own.

If your father is an alcoholic, you may want to sit down and look at what behaviors you're willing to be around and which you aren't. You may want to join Al-Anon or a group for Adult Children of Alcoholics.

If your sister has been gnashing her teeth over a divorce for six years now, refusing to let go and build a new life for herself, there may be a limit to how much you can take. You may want to have lunch with her once a month, but not be willing to take six midnight calls a week.

Your children may need the freedom to bicker, but you don't have to listen to it. Set up a Bickering Room. Shut them in there to bicker several hours a day, or make it available to them whenever they want.

The point is to see what you can do to make the situation work for you, regardless of their behaviors. This is a process of reaching down inside yourself and seeing what is important in your life.

4. *Be willing to create a life for yourself in this context.* This step is similar to the previous one, but includes a willingness to act on your possibilities. Sometimes it's hard to let go of being the martyr, the one whose life and opportunities have been limited by someone else. Some women are more comfortable being "golf widows" than finding an interest for themselves.

When people aren't willing to cause things to work for them, there is usually a payoff. They might get all sorts of attention and sympathy from their friends because of their plight. They might enjoy thinking of themselves as the "good" one who puts up with the "bad" one's behavior. They might be getting more out of the problems than the solutions.

Look at how you might be letting your family's behavior limit you, and at what you are willing to do about it. Do you consider time spent away from them as "dead time" in which you don't really do anything, and then resent them for wasting your time or being boring? Do you *make* enough time to be alone and do whatever you want to do? If someone in your family has a substance addiction, do you let it control your life? What can you do to create a fulfilling life for yourself, given that no one is going to change? Are you willing to do it?

5. *Discover your family's common bonds and interests, and capitalize on them.* Every family, biological or "chosen," needs common bonds and interests. Perhaps you are all devoted to a cause like world peace. You might be avid tennis players. You might be committed to personal growth. Perhaps you just enjoy being together and having the kinds of conversations that you do.

Suppose you marry someone, and two kids come along with the deal. You hadn't planned on having children or having any *more* children. What is your bond with them? Maybe it's just that all of you love the person you married.

At the very least, we all have the common bond of wanting to grow, to discover ourselves, accept life's challenges, and love one another. It's easier if people realize that this is what we all want, but it exists as a possibility for everyone.

This is another opportunity to get better acquainted with yourself and see what is important in your own life. What are your real interests and commitments? Are the ones with which you are occupied now really that important to you? Reexamine your commitments and see if it's possible to share them with your family. If it doesn't seem possible, look at what interests you *do* share.

6. *Choose whether or not you want to create intimacy within your biological family.* One reason people get so mired in family relationships is that they don't think they have a choice. They think, "This is my family, and I have to be close to them no matter how dreadful they are." This is simply not true. You don't have to spend the rest of your life slogging through relationships that you consider impossible.

Nor do you have to kick your family out of your life just because you don't think the possibility for intimacy exists with them. I know several people who are not intimate with their families, but who see them on a more casual basis. For one reason or another, intimacy was not possible, but they didn't want to sever the connection completely. They relate to their family by making themselves known to whatever extent they choose, and are willing to hear some of what their family says to them, but they don't punish themselves or their families because the relationships are not particularly intimate.

If you really don't think that the people in your biological family are people with whom you want to be intimate, give yourself permission to let go of that hope. It's no better to be intimate with your biological family than to be intimate with another group; it's just an option.

If you do want to create a climate for intimacy in your biological family, you are in a better position to do so if you have clearly chosen this path. You know what you are up against, you have a clearer idea of what is possible and what is not, and you can move ahead into the next level—commitment—with a firmer grasp of what you are doing.

For some families, the intimacy will be a very new and possibly threatening idea. It's usually best to come right out and tell people what you want to do, rather than holding intimacy as a hidden agenda and trying to trick people into it without their knowing. It's also best not to present it in a way that makes you seem like the enlightened one leading the unenlightened down the path to self-realization.

There is an inclination to be self-righteous about intimacy, to seem as if you know it all, as if you have all the answers and they've been doing it wrong all these years. It's usually better to come from the point of view that intimacy is something you want to do for yourself because you haven't been doing it, and that you would like their support. You might say something like, "I realize I haven't always been direct, and that there are things I haven't said. I'd like to begin saying those things, and hear anything you have to say, because I think it will make us closer." Then ask them how they feel about it. You may have made your choice, but they haven't necessarily made theirs. They may have no interest whatsoever in disrupting the homeostasis, telling the truth, making themselves known, hearing what you have to say, or realizing more of who they are. They may much prefer to keep things "polite" and not rock the boat.

You might also begin with just one member of the family. Sometimes it works to sit down at a "family council" and put out your idea to everyone at the same time, but it's usually easier with just one person at first.

While you're in the process of introducing intimacy into your biological family, it's often a good idea to get some outside support. It might be from Al-Anon or Adult Children of Alcoholics, church, a therapist, a women's support group, or friends with whom you are already intimate. It might simply be with your higher power. A spiritual foundation of some kind is very important when you begin this process. The Robots—both yours and your family's—are going to feel very threatened and get very active. You need a place or a person with whom you can remember the Spirit and stay in touch with why you are doing this.

Intimacy requires courage, and you're not likely to find all the support you need in your own family. They are new to this, after all. They may feel shaky and unsure of themselves at best, hostile and defensive at worst. In any case, they are not the people you should be counting on for support during this period of transition.

Committing to Intimacy in Your Biological Family

Once you have chosen to create intimacy in your biological family, you can go on to the next step—commitment. Your commitment to intimacy in your family is what keeps you going when the going gets tough. These are some guidelines to creating intimacy in your biological family:

1. *Clean the slate.* This may be the most uncomfortable, and the most important, step in creating intimacy. Cleaning the slate with your family means being willing to communicate everything you haven't communicated before, and being willing to hear what you haven't been willing to hear before. These things bring the relationship up to date and clarify it so you can see what is really going on.

Communicating everything you haven't communicated doesn't mean you have to tell them everything that has ever happened in your life. It just means telling them the things that are in the way of your being open to them. It means saying the things you've been avoiding, the things that make you bite your tongue, the things you're always thinking but not saying. Those are the things that get in the way, and they have to be handled before real intimacy can begin.

You also have to be willing to hear those things from them. Not only that, but you may have to be the one to create a receptive atmosphere for your family to say them. These things are often considered "impolite" and "inconsiderate." People are not accustomed to talking about them. What will make it "safe" for your family is your honest desire to hear them so that you can begin relating more intimately.

You need empty space in which to create. You need to get back to zero with your family so you can start anew. If your relationships with your family are filled with things from the past that are unsaid or unheard, there will be no space to start a new, intimate relationship.

Make a list of the things you need to say to each family member. What needs to be said or done? By what date will you have it done? If you knew you were going to die, what would feel incomplete or unfinished to you? What do you need to do or say in order to feel whole within yourself? What are the thoughts or issues that keep springing to mind over and over when you think about or spend time with your family? What are the old resentments and fears? These are the things that will repeat themselves in family relationships, or other relationships, again and again until you take care of them. You don't have to "fix" everything that is not working right away. Sometimes all you have to do is communicate about it.

This step is important even if you've chosen not to create intimacy in your biological family. If you leave issues and communications unresolved in your biological family, they will follow you everywhere you go. They will crop up in your "chosen" family, with friends, at work. You won't be able to move on to new issues and lessons until you complete them. But the most important reason to clean the slate with your biological family, even if you don't intend to be intimate with them, is your own peace of mind and the tremendous sense of relief that it brings.

Karen waited thirty-five years to clean the slate with her father. Her parents divorced when she was seven. Karen was devastated, but never told her father how she felt. She thought he might not want to see her even on weekends if she did. Her Robot made the decision: Men are untrustworthy and will leave you, but you can't say anything because that will just make it worse. Sure enough, every man whom Karen ever dated left her—for another woman, for a job out of town, because he needed "space," etc. She never communicated her anger to them, because she didn't want to look any worse than she already did and the relationship was over anyway. Her Robot was going to be "right" about that decision at any cost.

When she decided to let go of it, she told her father for the first time how hurt and angry she had been when he left. She didn't blame him for everything that had happened in her life; she just told him how she felt. He had known, of course, and was almost as relieved as she was that she had finally been able to tell him. His revelations allowed him to let go of some of his guilt, and helped Karen release a tightness and constraint she had always felt around men. She and her father never developed a really close relationship, but cleaning the slate made a difference in both of their lives.

For as long as she could remember, my friend Paula had felt on guard around her mother. Her mother had never approved of the men she dated, and she didn't approve of the man Paula married. Paula had been married to Dan for fifteen years, and every time she talked with her mother, the mother managed to work in some comment about Dan's perceived inadequacies. Paula got angry every time this happened, but she had done a lot of spiritual work and had decided that her mother's criticism was a test of her ability to stay serene in the midst of turmoil. Paula decided that her lesson was to "go with the flow," and "let it be," so she never told her mother how she felt.

Paula desperately wanted her mother's approval, and this was the real reason she never told her how she felt. Paula didn't want to lose what little she had with her mother, and was afraid the mother would lash back if Paula said anything negative. Her "spirituality" was a cover-up, a way to avoid conflict and at the same time feel superior to her mother.

When Paula chose to begin an intimate relationship with her mother, she had to start telling the truth. She had to tell her mother how she felt about criticism of Dan, and also about her fears and her need for approval. She said she wanted to let go of that need for approval so that she could continue to tell her mother what she was feeling. Her mother stared at her a moment, then said, "Well, that's fine, but I'll never approve of Dan. He's just not good enough for you, and it breaks my heart to see him ruining your life."

Paula loved Dan, but their relationship had all the normal ups and downs. Her mother's comments tended to shake Paula's confidence in the relationship, which was another reason she had suppressed her hurt and anger. The situation forced Paula to look again at her marriage, and to see that she wanted it despite the rocky times. She was able to tell her mother that, even though she knew her mother might use it as a weapon later.

The week after this conversation, Paula's mother was telling her about a wonderful house she'd seen for sale and ended the description with, "It would be just perfect for you, but of course on Dan's salary you could never afford it." Paula felt the anger well up, but was able to move beyond her Robot enough to say, "Mom, it really hurts me when you say things like that, and I get very angry. I want you to be able to tell me how you feel, and I understand that you don't think I should stay married to Dan, but I have to be able to tell you how I feel, too."

They went back and forth like this for a while, not agreeing but at least making themselves known to one another. It was uncomfortable, but Paula felt freer and more herself than she had in a long time. She saw that her newfound ability to tell her mother how she felt enabled her to let go of some of the hurt and anger.

After about a year, this dynamic simply ran out of steam. When Paula's mother didn't get any resistance to her criticism and began to feel heard, she became less interested in putting Dan down. There was nothing for her to push against, and so she stopped pushing. Paula began to see that her mother's criticism came out of love and concern. Since she had given herself permission to have and to communicate her honest responses, she could move on to something new.

Paula and her mother still have their different points of view, their different reactions and responses. Her mother still criticizes Dan occasionally, and Paula still gets upset sometimes, but their relationship is different now. Something has shifted, because they can tell the truth to one another. They also have all their cards on the table and know where they stand with one another.

At this point, the relationship is complete. The slate is clean. Tomorrow may bring another upset, but today Paula and her mother have said all there is to say. There is space for the relationship to move and change.

If Paula now wanted to go out and create a new family for herself, she could do so without re-creating this same pattern. She did what she needed to do with her mother, and she doesn't have to do it again. She might at some point want to create a relationship with someone outside her biological family that would be a little more supportive of her relationship with Dan, or she might not. When we tell the truth, all sorts of options become available. Regardless of what she does, Paula has discovered new parts of herself through her willingness to be intimate with her mother.

When I talk about cleaning the slate, people often say, "But my family members are no longer living. How can I complete my relationships with them?" There are many ways to do this. The family members don't have to be present physically. You just need to have the experience of communicating what you haven't communicated and hearing whatever the other person has not said.

One way to do this with a family member who has died is to sit down and look at a photograph of him or her for fifteen minutes without interruption. If possible, find a photo that lets you look into his or her eyes. Then say to that person everything you've ever wanted him to hear, out loud or in your mind. They may be things you've said before, but didn't feel were heard. Or maybe he or she did hear you, but you want to say them again.

Then look at the photo, and imagine that he is speaking to you. Let him tell you whatever he wanted you to know. This may be hard if it was a difficult relationship, because you may not want to hear what he says. He may say, "I did what I did because I love you," or "I just didn't know any other way of doing it." You may not want to hear that, but see if you can open up and let the communication in.

If you stay with this experience, at some point you will feel some kind of compassion for the person. No one has to be "right" or "wrong." The person's actions were human, and so were your responses. Everyone has a right to be human, but now it's time to forgive.

Another question people ask is, "How do I clean the slate when my family lives at the other end of the country?" If you are separated from your family by great distances and don't see them regularly, you have to use your time well. When you do have contact, allow yourself to be genuine. Watch your Robot's inclination to act the way it thinks these people want you to be. It's easier to slip back into old roles and patterns if you don't see your family often. It's also easy to see them in *their* old roles, and relate to them accordingly. Your Perfect Child sibling may be someone completely different now. Your Rebel brother may be a real straight arrow. Your mother may have joined the Gray Panthers and your

father taken up dirt biking. On the other hand, they may
have become *more* of who they were back then. Allow them
to show you who they are today.

There are always ways to extend yourself. You can
send cards and letters back and forth, call them occasionally,
and make an effort to stay in contact. Don't worry about
being creative. Sending cards, flowers, or candy may seem
mundane and "clichéd," but it's a beginning. The idea is to
connect.

2. *Tell the truth, even when it's risky.* This seems obvious,
but there is a tendency to ease off once a certain level of
intimacy has been established. It's easy to think, "Hey, we've
come this far. I don't want to rock the boat any more." After
the initial breakthrough, Paula told me she was often tempted
to let some of her mother's criticism go by without saying
how she felt about it.

There is something to this, in that we don't want to be
pushing people to the limit twenty-four hours a day. But it's
important to keep on track and to keep the communication
open. It's easy to become complacent, especially since the
process is so uncomfortable, and to fall into the trap of saying,
"Phew! I'm glad that's over with and I have this intimate
relationship. Now I can relax!"

We never get to the end of the road with intimacy. That's
one of the things that make it so interesting. Intimacy is
infinite, and we are infinite beings with infinite potential. We
will never discover all of our Spirit, because our Spirit is the
higher power, which is infinite. Intimacy isn't a place where
we arrive; it's a process that we live. There is always more
discomfort, more going beyond, more joy and more love—
no matter where we are.

3. *Be willing to keep hearing the truth.* This is the other side
of the coin. When someone has told us the thing they had
been unwilling to say before, we often heave a sigh of relief
that *that's* over. We forget to keep listening.

People will always have something to say to you, and their communication won't always be direct, clear, or compassionate. Remember how difficult communicating is for you sometimes, and recognize that for them it may be even more so.

Make a list of the people you suspect may have something to say to you, and give them the opportunity to do it. You don't have to buttonhole them and bully them into communicating, but make sure they know the space is available if they want to take it.

4. *Communicate directly.* Don't talk about your sister's problems with your mother, or your mother's problems with your sister—unless your purpose is to examine your *own* behavior, not theirs. It's possible to discuss one family member with other family members, and to concentrate on your own responses, but it's difficult not to fall into the trap of discussing "Joey's problem." Someone once said, "Communicate to someone who can do something about it."

Indirect communication is rarely productive, and can be particularly damaging in intimate relationships. Somehow the truth always comes out, and trust can be undermined. Your sister won't feel as good about revealing herself to you if she knows she's going to be the topic of conversation at lunch with your mother.

As an exercise, try for one month not talking about any family member with another. You'll be amazed at how often the temptation arises, and at how good it feels not to fall into this trap.

5. *Remember that everything communicates, all the time.* We are revealing ourselves all the time, whether or not we intend to do so. Other people may not understand everything we communicate on a conscious level, but they sense what is going on.

Communication isn't just the words we say. It can

be what we *don't* say, what we do or don't do, how we "seem" when we are with others or talking about certain subjects.

One evening, sit down and make a list of all the things you communicated that day without speaking, and of all the things that others communicated to you without speaking.

6. *Recognize that intimacy is a state you live in, not something you do every now and then.* Intimacy isn't something you can schedule in your datebook. It doesn't belong on your to-do list any more than brushing your teeth does. It's something that emerges out of who you are and what you want in life.

What *might* wind up on your to-do list is a thought about how to connect with someone, like sending a card or flowers. But intimacy is not something you can do without having it become a part of you. It is a process, not an event. It takes place over time, it grows and gets richer, and it feels more natural the more you eliminate the barriers to it.

Don't worry so much about whether you handled a particular situation "in an intimate way" as about how you feel about yourself, and how whole and honest and complete you feel with those around you. Give yourself some room to move and grow, some permission to develop intimacy rather than having to achieve it by a certain date.

You'll begin to know how much intimacy you have in your life by how you feel about yourself.

7. *Encourage those around you to follow these steps.* To encourage doesn't mean to nag. Literally, "encourage" means "to give heart to." It means to create an environment in which people feel free to be authentic.

I've heard it said that you never really have something until you give it away. Creating an environment in which other people feel good about being intimate with you is a way of giving it away, of sharing it so that it grows in the world and in your own heart.

8. *Be descriptive, not evaluative.* This is just another way of reminding you to communicate from Spirit, not Robot. The Robot evaluates everything—calls it good or bad, pretty or ugly, thoughtful or thoughtless. Rather than tell someone what they are or aren't, describe what happened, your reaction to it, and what you intend to do about it. Instead of saying, "Mom, there you go being critical again. When will you ever learn how much I hate that," say something like, "Mom, when you tell me my new hairdo looks like a fright wig, I get really angry. I feel put-down and belittled. Each time that happens I'm going to remind you that's how I feel."

9. *Keep communications current.* Effective communication is responsive, not reactive. It requires the ability to respond to the situation at hand, rather than react to it from past experiences. Responding means taking responsibility for communicating directly, in the moment. It means telling the truth. This doesn't mean you have to communicate every single thought or feeling you have, but it does mean to resist the temptation to let things slide and not say the things you know need to be said. Remember, if you let things build up, you're apt to go off like Vesuvius, dumping all kinds of things on some poor unsuspecting person.

Like intimacy, communication isn't something that happens once and then it's over. It's an ongoing process that takes some monitoring, especially at first.

There is no end to communication, any more than there is an end to intimacy. It is an ongoing process, something that becomes as much a part of life as breathing. Let it become a joy. Communication is the way we connect with other people, and ultimately with ourselves. It is the backbone of intimacy.

There are as many ways to choose and commit to intimacy in your biological family as there are families. In the next chapter, we will discuss another option: creating an entirely new family from among the people in your life.

THINGS TO DO

Make a list of evaluative words and phrases. Examples: good, bad, ugly, nice, cheap, thoughtless.

Write three sentences *describing* your reaction to someone's upsetting behavior. Example: "John, when you came home last night you slurred your words, staggered into the coffee table, and called me an old witch. I was, and am, extremely upset by your behavior. I know I can't baby-sit you every time you go out, but you cannot use the car until we have discussed this thoroughly and come to some very clear understanding."

List the people with whom you need to clean the slate.

Write down the essence of your communication for them. Take responsibility. Talk about yourself, not about them. Be descriptive, not evaluative.

CHAPTER SEVEN

HOW TO CREATE A "CHOSEN" FAMILY

We've been talking about the need for intimacy, and some of the ways you can bring it about in your existing family. We've explored what intimacy is and is not, the family dynamics of intimacy, and the fact that you get to initiate it unless you want to wait around forever until someone else does it. We've discussed Robots and Spirit, where intimacy breaks down, effective communication, how to clean the slate with your biological family, and, having done that, how to keep communication current.

Perhaps you have considered all of these issues, tried them out, and have come to the conclusion that it can't be done, or just isn't worth the effort with your existing family. It's important to know that there are alternatives.

Melinda is seventeen and has made a concerted effort to create a new family for herself. Born to a schizophrenic mother and father who took off when she was eight, Melinda grew up in a confusing atmosphere. Shunted from relative to relative, and then back to her mother, Melinda never felt certain of anything. Untimately, she ended up as a ward of the court. Befriended by a classmate, Trish, the court finally allowed Trish's parents to become Melinda's foster family.

Wanting to ensure that communication got off to a good start, Trish's parents brought the family to see me. Melinda was fourteen at the time. Not surprisingly, Melinda's Robot was operating in full force. Frightened of being rejected once again, Melinda would hide out in her bedroom and suck her thumb. Not wanting to upset the applecart and scared to death of being disliked, she would refuse to express any negative thoughts or feelings and then erupt in a tearful rage over seemingly petty issues, like the time Trish borrowed a hair ribbon without asking. Over time, however, Melinda was able to understand her reactions: where they came from, what triggered them, and ultimately, how to control them without stuffing them.

She began to apply the principles we've explored so far in this book and created a new family for herself, not only with Trish and her parents but also with other friends.

Melinda loves her biological mother and still visits her with some frequency. But she understands that her mother's illness precludes the kind of constancy that Melinda needs in her life right now. She is no longer ashamed of her background or of sucking her thumb. And so, having nothing to hide, she is truly on the road to creating intimate and fulfilling relationships in her life.

Like Melinda, if you don't feel that you can experience intimacy in your biological family, it may be time to consider creating a family with whom you *can* be intimate. This doesn't mean you have to sever connections with your biological family; it just means that there is a level of intimacy you want in your life that isn't being provided there, and you want it in a new family.

It's important to remember that this is not an easy process. It's going to take time and effort on your part, and a commitment to experiencing things you have been trying to avoid, like loneliness or low self-esteem, for example. Nothing can make you feel more lonely or unworthy than admitting you'd like to be with someone, making a stab at it, being rejected, and finding yourself still alone. But in this case the old cliché "Nothing ventured, nothing gained" is true. You may have to take five or ten stabs at it. Your choices may be to go on feeling a sort of low-grade loneliness forever, or experiencing some real heavy doses of rejection and giving yourself a chance to get past it.

There are no guarantees in life, and intimacy and friendship are no exceptions to the rule. But here are the odds: If you don't take a chance, your life will go on as it has been, and probably get worse the older you get. If you do take a chance, the odds are at least fifty-fifty that you'll win. In fact, they're better than that, because you'll increase your self-esteem simply by summoning the courage to act. The rewards of making the effort are clearly worth it, as my client Melinda will attest.

Why Create a New Family?

There are many circumstances that might prompt you to create a new family for yourself. These are only a few:

1. *Your biological family is no longer living.* You may have had wonderful relationships with the people in your biological family and miss them very much. Occasionally, people feel it might be disloyal to their deceased family if they went out and created a new one. But in the end, these people know their families would want them to be happy and to find new people with whom to share their lives. It's important to go through the grieving process, but it is also important not to close yourself off from other people because your biological family has died.

2. *You have been "divorced" from your biological family.* For whatever reason, your biological family may not want you in their lives or you may not want them in yours. This might be due to alcoholism, the "wrong" marriage, an admission of homosexuality, disagreements about money, or anything that breaks the family apart. These things are painful, and there are times when we just aren't in a position to heal them. We can, however, get over the belief that we have to "make it" with our biological family in order to experience the joys of intimacy. We have to remember that these difficulties are there to teach us lessons, and that maybe one of the lessons is to move away from a situation that has become abusive.

3. *The relationship with your biological family is intact but not intimate.* Sometimes it is just not in the cards to experience intimacy with your biological family. I have a friend who introduced the idea of intimacy to her mother and received the response, "I wouldn't want to do that at all. If I started exploring like that and telling the truth, I'd have to leave your father and it wouldn't be worth it. I've lived like this for sixty years and I don't want to dig up all that muck now."

This is a clear choice, and an honest one, but it doesn't leave much room for intimacy. My friend wanted intimacy in her life, and so chose to create a new family. She still wanted to keep contact with her mother, but realized that the relationship would never be much more than polite.

4. *You simply want to expand the quality and quantity of intimacy in your life.* You can have rich, intimate relationships within your biological family and still want to create more intimate relationships. I love my family deeply and have intimate relationships with them, but I also like to have other intimate friendships. I have a professional mentor who is like a surrogate aunt, a dancer friend who is like a sister, and several other close relationships apart from my family. Rather than distancing me from my own family, they make those relationships even richer.

Reaching Out

It's going to take guts, and maybe that's what you were afraid of. But the fact is, sitting home and waiting for someone loving, kind, thoughtful, and compassionate with an overwhelming capacity for intimacy to show up at your doorstep is ridiculous.

Hackneyed as it may sound, you have to get up, get out, and go where the people are if you're going to have friends—much less intimacy.

Your reason for creating a new family doesn't matter as much as your desire to do it. If you want it, it's there for you to have.

Some people say, "Oh, why would so and so be interested in *me*? I don't have much to offer." Usually, what these people really mean is, "I don't think other people have much to offer *me*."

Intimacy has to be based on some sort of common interest or concern. If you're not interested in anything or committed to anything, it's going to be hard. If we have nothing in our lives that is pushing us, challenging us, contributing to our growth and expansion, we aren't going to have much to be intimate *about*. Certainly, the first step toward finding new intimates is knowing what your interests and commitments are.

Maybe your interest is in astronomy. Get together with a few people, or even one person at a time, and talk about the stars. It won't be your knowledge of the constellations that creates the intimacy; it will be your willingness to become known to one another. But the stars are a common area of interest that you can talk about in the process. "Common" is the key word. You won't meet many Republicans while licking envelopes for Democrats.

Often it takes time to develop these relationships. You can't always just walk into a situation and have everyone welcome you with open arms. You may have to hang out for a while so that people get used to you before you can start creating relationships. Sandi's aerobics class has become a kind of family to her, but it took a year before she really felt at home there and comfortable enough just asking people out to lunch.

Michele came to see me because she wasn't meeting any men. Upon investigation, I discovered she never went anywhere to meet men, because she'd gone to a couple of singles bars and had two or three blind dates and they were disastrous experiences. What Michele didn't understand was the nature of determination.

Nothing much gets done without determination. Great music doesn't get written, gymnastics championships aren't won, books aren't written, and relationships aren't created without someone determining that they will happen.

Determination requires the willingness to commit to something, to leave no stone unturned, to try whatever must be tried. Robots have many reasons for not trying things, and they can be used interchangeably for many situations. "I don't have time" to write a book, go to a square dance, call a friend. "I'd be embarrassed," "I'm not confident enough," "I'd look foolish," "I might be bored." The list goes on and on.

But if you are going to succeed at anything, you have no choice but to give it all you've got. The results will begin to appear in the most surprising ways. Michele finally gave up her excuses for not meeting people. She began to try everything, including dating clubs, the Audubon Society, and volunteering for a political candidate.

One day she was standing in line at the post office and struck up a conversation with the man standing next to her. They were married six months later.

Perhaps they would have met anyway, but Michele's not sure she would ever have seen him, much less had the nerve to talk to him, had she not been putting herself out in so many other ways.

You can't count on other people to make the first move. Finding the courage to extend yourself may be as rewarding as the intimacy itself. This is true whether you are looking for new friends or trying to reconnect with old friends.

Moira and Adeline had been business partners, but had had a terrible falling out. They didn't speak to one another for years. As time healed some of the hurt, Adeline realized that, while she might not want to go into business with Moira again, she loved her and wanted to be her friend. It was their friendship that had prompted them to go into business together in the first place. She called Moira and suggested they get together for coffee. That was hard for her to do, and a hard invitation for Moira to accept, but gradually they were able to talk about what had happened and to reestablish their friendship. It took time, and a lot of extending themselves to one another when they were afraid of being hurt, but now they are like sisters.

Choosing People

Once you have a few people in your life, old or new, spend some time looking at who you might want to become your family. You can choose certain people for certain roles—mother, father, brother, sister—or you can simply assemble a group without particular roles. Sooner or later, the roles will emerge as they do in any group.

Choose people with whom intimacy is a possibility. They don't all have to be experts in interpersonal dynamics, but there should be some kind of openness to the idea of intimacy. You might be fighting a losing battle if you choose people who are generally closed and give no indication of wanting to grow. Make sure this is something that they want as much as you do.

You might begin simply by spending more time with them or by upgrading the quality of time you spend with them. Let them see you in ways they haven't before, and make room for them to do the same.

Extend yourself. It's hard sometimes, but people love it. They may be shy themselves and not warm up to you right away, but think about how you feel when people extend themselves to you. You want to respond, even if it takes you a while. The people you approach do already have lives they are leading. Sometimes they are reticent to add new "obligations." It will take some time to adjust old habits and commitments to include this new friendship. But be patient. Give it some time to flourish. It's a little like waiting for a flower to bloom. Once it has done so, the waiting was worth it.

You can see the glass as half empty or as half full. You can get lost in the fear or realize that you are offering people an opportunity to relate to you, the opportunity for intimacy that we all want more than anything else. It may not be comfortable, but it is enlivening and richly rewarding.

Creating Your Own Family

This can be the greatest adventure of your life. Here are some exercises that will help you choose and create a whole new family for yourself:

1. *Tell yourself the truth about the fact that you have no family.* This is true whether your biological family is no longer living, whether there has been some rift with them, or whether you simply don't have intimacy with them. If you do have an intimate relationship with your biological family and simply want *more* intimacy, then tell the truth about that.

Sometimes we realize intellectually that we have no family or that we don't have an intimate family, but we don't let ourselves really feel the anger, grief, guilt, or homesickness that comes with the loss. If you've come from a terrible family of emotional axe murderers and have chosen to leave it, your initial feeling might be one of relief and happiness that you don't have to deal with them any longer. But deep down may be some loss and grief, if only at your pictures of what might have been.

2. *Let go.* You also have to give up the dream that your family might ever change and that the situation might transform into something wonderful. To have a new family, you have to give up something of the old.

Let go of your old family and any pictures or feelings you may have about it. When people try to create a family on the old models from their biological families, they usually run into trouble. The new family becomes dysfunctional to whatever extent the old one was. The new "mother" inexplicably becomes a nag, the new "sister" a whiner, the new "brother" rebellious and troublesome.

Some people feel a desperate need to get the new family together as quickly as possible. To cut corners, they try to become part of a family that already exists, without laying any groundwork, or they try to manipulate what are actually casual friendships into family situations. They can't understand when they get rebuffed. They *tried* to create a family; there must be something wrong with the other people—or with them.

Letting go gives you the empty space you need in order to create your new family.

3. *Recognize that there are still lessons to be learned.* If you have "unfinished business" with your biological family, it will resurface in your "chosen" family. If your mother's criticism used to drive you nuts, there will almost certainly be a critical person in your new family. The same kinds of roles and dynamics will recur unless you have come to terms with them. This shouldn't be looked at as a bad development, but rather as life giving you a chance to learn your lessons and complete what you need to complete.

The difference in your new family may be that people have come together with common understanding of their desire to be intimate, to reveal themselves to one another in a safe environment, to hear one another's Robots, and then to move on through their commitment to Spirit. If that's something you want in your new family, it is best to make it known as soon as possible.

One advantage we have in a "chosen" family is that patterns have not been built up over the years. Another is that we may be older and wiser than we were with our biological families. Presumably, we've gained some knowledge and experience from our dealings with our blood families, and are in a better place to cope with upsets when they occur—even when these upsets closely resemble situations that came up in our biological families.

You can rechoose not only how you handle the situation but also the type of people you have around you. If your mother was an unrecovered alcoholic and that resulted in all sorts of problems for you and for the family, you don't have to have an unrecovered alcoholic in your "chosen" family. But choosing a recovered one could help you unmake some old decisions. The lesson may have been that you don't have to put up with certain behaviors. You are not necessarily running away from trouble when you choose people who are different from the people in your biological family. If you *haven't* learned the lesson, it will find you no matter how far you run.

4. *Clean the slate with your biological family.* This process is detailed in the previous chapter. Essentially, it means saying to them all the things that are incomplete and need to be said, and hearing from them everything that is incomplete with them and needs to be heard. They don't have to be there with you in person for you to do this. Some of the exercises in the previous chapter show how to clean the slate even with family members who are no longer living.

If your relationship with your biological family has been very difficult, you may just want to say good-bye to them and get on with your life. The last thing you may want to do is clean the slate and root around in all the uncomfortable issues they bring up for you. But you must do it because the purpose of cleaning the slate is to complete the past so you can move on to the future. If you don't do it, those people and issues will be rattling around in the back of your mind forever and reappear in every other relationship you have. You can't begin a new family with old resentments, anger, and guilt cluttering up the space.

The process of cleaning the slate with your biological family helps you and everyone around you. At the very least, you release some old negativity. That may open up the opportunity for other family members to do the same.

5. *Take some time off to enjoy your freedom.* You may want to take some time for yourself before you enter into the process of creating a new family. There may be things you've always wanted to do, or new opportunities you're only likely to take if you are alone. You no longer have to worry about some of the old problems, and you no longer have some of the old responsibilities. As you develop new relationships, some of the old issues may arise to be confronted. You can face that when it happens. Right now, however, you probably have more free time. Maybe you've always wanted to take a trip to Europe or go see three movies a week. Maybe this is the time to fix a turkey dinner for yourself with the kind of dressing *you* like.

Be creative with your new freedom. This can be a tremendously exciting time—one in which you find new parts of yourself, new things to enjoy in the world, and new people with whom to share both.

Dale was thirty-three and lived in Chicago. Every Christmas, he found himself trudging down to southern Illinois to be with his family. He watched his father get drunk at Christmas dinner, listened to his mother nag him about not being married, and put up with his sister's children screaming all through dinner, squirming around on his lap and rubbing turkey gravy into his new sweater. He found it all terribly uncomfortable, and one year he told his family how he felt. He didn't mention the turkey gravy, but he did say he thought he needed a break from the family and had some friends

with whom he wanted to spend the holidays. He didn't sever
the relationship. He simply made known to them how he felt
at Christmas and said he wouldn't be coming home that year.

The week before Christmas, as he was walking down
Michigan Avenue with all the lights twinkling in the trees
and carols being sung on every corner, Dale had some twinges
of homesickness and guilt. He almost decided to go home
after all, but he stuck with his choice and made an effort to
enjoy his new freedom. He called his friends and made plans
to go skiing in Aspen. He had a few more twinges on Christmas Day, but on the whole he thoroughly enjoyed the trip.
Even more, he enjoyed knowing that he had freedom and
choices. And most of all, he was excited and ready to go
home the next year, even if he had to experience his family's
hurt feelings for a while.

6. *Explore what "family" really means to you.* Now you have
the space and the freedom to create. You've cleaned the slate
with your biological family, let go of them, experienced all the
feelings that go along with that, and enjoyed your freedom.

Before you actually start creating your new family, take
some time to explore what family means to you and exactly
what you want to create. What comes to mind when you think
of family? Does it mean people who are there for you in an
emergency? Does it mean having people in your life whom
you can just call up every day and say hi to? People to live
with and share your life? People with whom to go places?
People with whom you can sit and say nothing? Bridge or
tennis partners?

Family means different things to different people. You
can set it up any way you want. Some of the things it means
to me are people with whom I can take a five-hour drive and
say two words, with whom I don't have to be entertaining or
smart, with whom I don't have to be or do *anything*. My family
are people who tell me when I'm getting out of line, and with
whom I can do the same. They are people who want to
experience their connections with the higher power more

than anything, and who aren't afraid of their own humanness—or mine—as it presents itself along the way.

You might even want to sit down and make a list of all the things that family means to you. This is a slippery subject, one about which we're likely to make assumptions that may or may not be accurate, one that may be hard to pin down and make concrete. The clearer you are about what you want, the more likely you are to get it. I saw a poster once that read, "If you don't know where you're going, you're likely to wind up somewhere else."

7. *Create your new family out of common bonds, interests, and commitments.* In the process of opening yourself up to new possibilities, you may have discovered some new interests and commitments in life. The place to look for family is where your interests and commitments are.

It's difficult for a family to exist without common bonds and commitments. If you don't have much in common when you start out, you will probably want to create some interests you can share. The common bonds and commitments don't have to be serious and weighty. Your commitment can be simply to creating a home environment that nurtures all of you, to discovering yourselves through intimacy, to deepening your connection with your higher power.

It is these bonds, and your commitment to one another, that will carry you through the hard parts and give your relationships a meaning beyond themselves.

8. *Stick your neck out.* Even if you are a gregarious, outgoing person, you become vulnerable when you make the first move. People might not respond, or might not respond the way you want them to. Still, you can't sit home and hope that a new family just shows up at your door.

Sticking your neck out means not only meeting new people but expanding the level of intimacy with the friends you already have. Sometimes that can be just as uncomfortable. Take it slowly. Allow the relationship to grow over time, revealing more and more of yourself naturally and allowing the other person to do the same.

Some circumstances call for some extra creativity and initiative to do this. One woman who lost her voice made up a board game for her family to play based on revealing themselves to one another to help her keep up the communication and intimacy.

Intimacy is something you are doing for yourself. Regardless of the other person's response, revealing yourself to them is a process of self-discovery. The worst that can happen is that you know yourself better and discover more of who you are.

9. *Create a history with your new family.* Traditional biological families have a built-in history. We've lived with these people over a period of years. We've shared ups and downs, family outings, holidays, tragedies, happy moments, births and deaths, and all the "little things" of life as well. We know who likes peas and who hates broccoli, who won the three-legged sack race in 1972. We know about Aunt Sarah's arthritis and Uncle Arthur's Medal of Honor. These things bind us together, whether or not they seem particularly positive.

Some people are afraid they will never have this kind of history with anyone else. Again, it's a matter of choice. In a "chosen" family, we have to make a conscious effort to create these histories. Holidays, when everyone is dressed up and well behaved, are not enough. We need to plan picnics, ball games, evenings of card playing, outings to the park or the movies, pumpkin carving, Easter egg dyeing, etc. These activities might not be important in themselves, but they give us a chance to be together and participate, to find out the little things about one another and create memories that we can share. We need to make the effort to invite people over for Monday night football or *Richard III* on television, to ask people if they would like to go to the country with us this weekend, to volunteer to make soup if someone is sick and, just as important, to let people make soup for *us*. It may seem awkward at first, but histories are important.

My friend June is about fifty. Her parents died years ago, and she is divorced with no children. The one relative with whom she was close, an elderly aunt, died recently. June decided that she wanted to create a new family with whom to share her life, and very consciously set about doing so.

A male friend became her brother, I became her sister, and she found various other people who wanted to enter into other types of family relationships with her. It didn't happen overnight, and it required some attention. She and I had to develop the kind of relationship in which we could say what we didn't like without being afraid that the other would leave. June had to create a history with her new family, the kinds of things like shared holidays, ball games, and popcorn by the fire that happen naturally over the years in biological families.

In doing this, it's important to remember that people in your "chosen" family won't always live up to your highest expectations, any more than your biological family did. You might, for instance, invite everyone in your "chosen" family over for Thanksgiving dinner or Christmas. You like to do this, but after a while it occurs to you that you are always the one doing the inviting and making the dinners. You wonder why they don't invite *you* over for a change.

In biological families, there is often one person who always winds up having the holiday dinners at her house. Someone fills that caretaker role, whether it's Grandma or Aunt Clara, of making sure the family gets together. And you may be that person in your "chosen" family. If that doesn't suit you, be creative. If you don't always want to do the cooking, make the dinners potluck. Or ask someone else to have the dinner at their house and promise to help with the cooking. You may still be the organizer, the planner, but you can say, "How about if we met at your house next time?"

Sometimes we get the notion that because our biological families did certain wonderful things, our new families should naturally do the same kinds of things. But "chosen" family members need to be able to say no. You can't let your nose get out of joint if you call people up to go to a movie and they don't want to go. They need the freedom to tell you that they just don't feel like going out that night, just as the members of your biological family might.

Co-workers Are Not Family

The principles in this book are applicable to all relationships. Robots operate everywhere. They're not exclusive to family. Learning to communicate from the Spirit is valuable at the grocery store as well as Christmas dinner. Stuffing and dumping don't work any better on the salesperson than they do on your mother. And group dynamics are as evident in the boardroom as they are in the dining room. And so applying these principles of roles, communication, groups, and intimacy will be helpful in the workplace, with but one admonition: Do not make the mistake of trying to create a family at work. It's great to have a familylike atmosphere in the office, but it almost never works to make these people your primary source of support and intimacy.

The workplace is by definition a place devoted to survival issues. People go there to earn money so they can survive. Everyone may be happy and jolly, but if you threaten someone's job, you are threatening that person's livelihood and, ultimately, his life. To some extent, everyone has to be concerned about what the boss thinks. The boss, in turn, has to worry about *his* boss. The company has to worry about other companies. Its purpose is to beat out the competition and survive in the world of business. There are very few aspects of the workplace that are not about survival of one kind or another.

I found this out in a very personal way when I left home at the age of seventeen to join the New York City Ballet Company. As a member of a ballet company, it's extremely difficult to have "outside" friends. Not too many "normal" people are free when you are—evenings at 11:30, or Mondays, your one day off. The company becomes your life. And when you're on tour you really have no escape.

So the other members of the company become your friends, your lovers, your family. At the same time, a ballet company is rife with survival issues over roles, attention from the director, weight problems, jealousies, and relationships. Robots are rampant.

Young and inexperienced, I made "best" friends with several members of the company. It was a disaster—especially when my very best friend turned on me for getting a role she desperately wanted.

You may find familylike situations at work, but they will most likely mimic the dynamics of families that are focused on survival. Families focused on survival are dysfunctional families. The relationships within them are dependent. This might be fine on a limited basis, but it's not the kind of dynamic you want at the center of your life.

It might be fine for Carla the secretary to go into work each day and play Charmer at the office, to primp and croon and enjoy having everyone think how cute she is. She may have fun with that role if she doesn't get identified with it and start believing it's who she is. For all her boss knows, she goes home and runs her family with an iron hand. She may actually be tough as nails, betting the horses and playing the stock market so that someday she can tell him to take this job and shove it.

In the workplace, everybody needs something. There is certainly no way you can reveal yourself if your survival—emotional or economic—is dependent on another person's response to you. If you need that job, or that raise, or that promotion, then it is very difficult to establish intimacy.

Even if you have reached a point, financially and otherwise, that you don't need the job, you still can't guarantee that others won't need *their* jobs and treat you accordingly.

We've all known or heard about the person who honestly

believes her co-workers are her family, but then is left out in the cold on holidays and vacation time. Everyone is her great friend at work, but when push comes to shove, they all go home to their own *real* families and don't make room for her.

This is not to say that you can't be close to the people with whom you work, or that you can't have caring relationships with them. You can. It's just important to keep some perspective and to understand that this is a survival situation, that the circumstances can change very quickly, and that the workplace is not the best place to invest your primary support and intimacy.

One of the wonderful things about creating a family for yourself is that you can have relationships that aren't always possible in biological families. Having been a professional ballet dancer, I love to include people from the dance world in my family.

I also think it's nice to have new family members with interests different from mine, and I've learned a great deal from my mother, who has mastered this kind of relationship beautifully. She has consciously developed her friendships with three other ladies her own age, and they are like a family, even though she has close relationships with her children and her grandchildren. These three ladies are all in their eighties, and they get together regularly to play cards and tennis. They always spend New Year's Eve together, and turn down invitations from their biological families to do so. They have taken on roles—one is the caretaker, one is the quiet one, and one is the Charmer. They act out the roles in a delightful and nonthreatening way, and everyone gets to do what she does best. My mother is very smart; she's not going to end up old and alone, and she's not going to end up with just her children and grandchildren, all of whom have their own lives. I'm trying to be just as smart as she is, and am consciously developing relationships with people my own age that we can enjoy as we grow older.

You don't have to give up your biological family in order to add and balance out with a "chosen" family. I have my biological family, my ballet family, my professional family, and a number of people who are such good friends they have become like sister and brother.

The Reward

Creating your own "chosen" family can be exhilarating. It is a possibility that is more available to us now than it ever has been in history. For many, it is a necessity and can mean the difference between loneliness and a joyous sharing of life. For others, it is a way to expand what is already a high level of intimacy.

In any case, it is an opportunity to discover more of yourself by making yourself known to others and allowing them to make themselves known to you, and to deepen your connection with your higher power. It is also a great deal of fun. It's like falling in love over and over—with yourself and with other people.

QUESTIONS TO ASK YOURSELF

Who are my intimate friends?
Whom would I like to know better?
What are my interests?
With whom do I share those interests?
What new interests would I like to develop?

THINGS TO DO

Invite a close friend to lunch or dinner.
Participate in a new activity.
Invite a new friend to go on a picnic or to a movie.
Invite four friends or acquaintances over for a potluck.

CHAPTER EIGHT

SPECIAL FAMILIES

Nontraditional families used to be the exception; now they are becoming the norm. It is important for step families, gay families, single-parent families, families in which both parents work, and other types of nontraditional families to be aware of their special needs. These families often face greater challenges, and as a result have even greater opportunities for intimacy.

Families with special circumstances are often subject to more stress. The same dynamics apply as in more traditional families, but they are more pronounced. Since the survival of the family depends to some extent on its acceptance by society, survival issues are more likely to be raised in special families.

The family in which one or more people are addicted to a substance is an extreme example. Everything is exaggerated. The fights are louder; the roles are more rigid; the problems seem bigger; the fear for survival is stronger. The family's dysfunction can't be hidden, and so something is more likely to be done about it. Other families may be just as dysfunctional as the addicted family, but because the problems seem more subtle and the conversation is more polite, the issues never get handled.

This is why so many people from nonaddicted families are involved in groups for Adult Children of Alcoholics, whose purpose is to serve people who grew up in alcoholic homes. Many people grew up in homes *without* alcoholics that were just as dysfunctional, but because things looked so much better on the surface, the wheel never got oiled. I have a friend who kept hearing about and identifying with the symptoms of adult children of alcoholics. She couldn't figure it out because her parents didn't appear to have any problems with alcohol. Then she realized that dysfunction is dysfunction, whether it is expressed in throwing dishes around the living room or sitting quietly at the dining table making polite conversation.

The differences between addicted families and the special families we will discuss in this chapter is that addicted families are, by definition, dysfunctional and the special families we will discuss are not. They may *become* dysfunctional, just as any family can, but they can just as easily find a high level of intimacy.

Special families have tremendous opportunities. The stakes are higher. The dynamics are more intense. Intimacy has to be chosen, created consciously, and nurtured. Frankly, that gives these families a better chance for intimacy—if they are willing to work on it. Let's look at five examples.

1. *Step families.* Say you marry someone who already has children. You want this person and the marriage, but suddenly you have a whole new family and begin to realize that there are going to be some problems. These kids have a history with a parent other than you, and you realize you don't have the same feelings for them that you might if they were your own children. What are your options? How can you develop intimacy with these youngsters, who don't even seem like they want you around, let alone want to be intimate with you?

The principles of creating intimacy are the same: making yourself known to them and being willing to have them make themselves known to you. One of the things your stepchildren may want you to know is that you are *not their parent*. They will communicate this to you in many ways, some subtle and some strikingly obvious. They may totally ignore you and act as if you don't even exist. They may disobey you deliberately and dare you to say anything to them. If you do correct or discipline them, they may say, "You can't say things like that to me. You're not my parent. You can't tell me what to do."

If their other parent is alive, they usually hope that this other parent and your spouse will get back together. They may blame *you*, because now that you are married, it seems impossible. Even if you come into the picture years after their parents have separated, they may resent you because they will "never be a family again."

If you and your spouse have your own child, the situation gets even more complex. You're likely to spend more time with the new child, if only because he or she is a baby. You may feel guilty for not spending as much time with your stepchildren. Rest assured that they will realize this and find a way to use it.

When all these elements are added to the family dynamic, you have to strive for intimacy at a much more conscious and responsible level. You need to know your own motivations and intentions well, and make them known both to your spouse and to the children.

You may need to communicate to your spouse that you don't have the authority you need with the children, the authority you would have if you were their biological parent, and that you want his or her help. He or she might have been thinking of taking a little vacation from responsibility for the children now that you're around, and be disappointed or even angry that you don't want to step in and take care of everything yourself. You may have to tell your spouse that his or her presence is even more important now because you are a new component in the family dynamic.

If your new spouse is the children's mother, her attitude may be, "Whew! Now this man can discipline these kids for me." If you are "this man," you may feel that you are expected to save the day by being heavy-handed. You may have watched these kids manipulate their mother for the past three years, and now you have a chance to do something about it. If you step in and become the disciplinarian without the children's permission, you may cause alienation that lasts a long time.

This is particularly true with older children. Stepparents can move into a parental role fairly easily with small children, but by the time they reach the age of five or six they may not be as willing to accept the stepparent's authority.

In either case, the biological parent must be *more* present and the communication *more* clear and caring, more intimate.

Parents believe they should have control over their children, but the fact is that children have tremendous power over adults, especially in a society which demands that parents prove they are "good parents." This gives kids a lot of ammunition, and the situation is aggravated when it's not a parent but a stepparent who is involved.

We still have images of the "wicked stepmother," and now we've added the image of the stepfather as a child molester. Stepparents not only have to prove that they are "good parents," they have to prove that they are not wicked ones. The stepchildren's ammunition is now almost limitless. All they have to do is upset and disobey the stepparent, and they have proved that the stepparent has no control over them. They have this new person just where they want him.

Tension rises between the parents as well. It's hard to hear people criticize your biological child, especially if they start making comparisons with their biological children. Steve had a five-year-old boy and Joyce a five-year-old girl when they married. The girl tended to cry easily and be hypersensitive. The little boy had a "cute" racket and could manipulate his father into almost anything. Steve had a lot of trouble dealing with this whiny, hypersensitive little girl. Joyce couldn't bear to watch this little boy manipulate his father and try to manipulate her.

Neither Steve nor Joyce wanted to criticize the other's child, and neither wanted to hear any criticism in return. Instead, they communicated indirectly. Instead of saying, "I think your little boy is very manipulative," Joyce would just roll her eyes, sigh, and get a certain superior look on her face whenever the little boy acted up. Steve rolled his eyes whenever the little girl cried.

Tremendous tension built up in all the relationships. By the time they realized what was happening, Steve and Joyce were caught up in the web their children had woven for them. They had to sit down and do their best to form a team. They had to tell the truth to each other about their fears and apprehensions as stepparents and make some choices about how they were going to handle the kids. They realized that the alternative was breaking up, which may have been exactly what the kids had in mind, and they didn't want to do that.

Being in a step family requires some attention and some conscious creation of intimacy. There is less room for the Robot, which is difficult, because the Robot is likely to be even more active and more troublesome in stressful situations. But of course, the more you become aware of your Robot, the less control it has over you.

In creating a step family, you have made conscious choices to be with certain people. What's necessary to make it work is the commitment to those choices, the willingness to keep revealing yourself and letting others do the same, an increasing awareness of your Robot, and a choice for the Spirit. This means being patient while people jostle for position, do some testing, and establish trust. This family may never look like the "ideal," but there is tremendous joy and exhilaration in creating intimacy within a step family. You have all come together from different places and perhaps experienced some difficulties along the way, but you have made it through—and you have made it together.

2. *Gay Families.* In many cases, gay families are also step families. More and more gay couples are adopting or having their own children, but most gay parents are still stepparents.

Again, the dynamics are the same as in traditional families—but there is the stress involved in being a step family, and the added stress of being a family that doesn't get a lot of approval from society. Once again, the roles, dynamics, and everyone's "robotics" are exaggerated.

In gay families, the children's other biological parent may have trouble dealing not just with the separation, but with the issue of homosexuality. So may one or both spouses' parents and family. The children may grow up separated from their extended families because the gay parent isn't accepted.

There may also be confusion when the children's friends come over after school. Even if the friends aren't confused, their parents may be. How this is received will depend upon the people involved, and perhaps upon the area of the country where you live. In San Francisco, it might not be a problem. In other areas of the country, it might be.

In my experience, the children of gay families are at least as healthy as children of more traditional families, and possibly more so. Perhaps they have an advantage because they learn early how important it is to know and accept who they and the people they love are. Their parents have had to confront themselves, often in very painful and memorable ways, and the strengths they've gained as a result are apt to be apparent to their children early in life.

I read once that "sanity is the ability to perceive things from another's perspective." Children of gay families learn early to see things from another's perspective and to accept things that are quite different from what most other people accept. They are inclined to be more tolerant and accepting of people who are different from them, and to choose friends based on who people are, rather than on their circumstances.

People say, "If they grow up in a gay environment, they'll be gay." This is demonstrably untrue. They will be however they are. Children who grow up in gay families show no more statistical likelihood of being gay than people who grow up in heterosexual families. When I have seen unhealthy or dysfunctional situations in gay homes, it's almost always the result of some other dynamic or addiction, and has nothing to do with homosexuality.

Some of the best relationships between parents and children I've seen have been in gay homes where the parents' homosexuality is out in the open and being dealt with directly. It's almost as if the parents have nothing left to hide. They have claimed who they are in a society that doesn't necessarily approve, and are dealing with the consequences. They have told their children, whose love they want most. Having taken these risks and come to know themselves much better in the process, the atmosphere at home is likely to be more open and relaxed. All the secrets have already been told. In many cases, the children have watched their parents go through this process and learned from it.

In homes where the parents are trying to hide their homosexuality—from the children and everyone else—there can be tremendous tension. It's difficult to make yourself known to anyone, including yourself, when you can't reveal one of the most basic things about yourself, the way you love.

Other people are "out of the closet," but are still defensive. They feel they have to justify it, rationalize it, sometimes to the exclusion of other things in their lives. Imagine a father whose stance was, "I'm a *steelworker*, by God, and proud of it! I know you don't like it, but that's too bad. That's what I am, and you can go to hell!" However, most gay people who choose to have families have come to terms with their homosexuality. There seems to be some sort of groundwork laid by "coming out" that makes it easier to be intimate.

Gay parents have usually had to do quite a bit of self-exploration. They need strong internal structures and a connection with something more than their homosexuality in order to survive in a disapproving society. That puts them ahead of the game when it comes to intimacy, and is something they are inclined to pass on to their children.

In my observation, the most difficult issues in gay families are usually the step family issues. Other than that, gay families may actually have a clearer road to intimacy than some straight families.

3. *Single-Parent Families.* The difficulty here is one of sheer exhaustion. Most single parents work, and they also take care of their children without the help and support of a spouse. Many feel they are on a treadmill. It's hard to think about being intimate with anyone, least of all children, when you are dead on your feet. On the other hand, intimacy is not something you sit down and *do.* It's not a matter of how many hours you put in or how many discussions you have. A simple willingness to be yourself and let others do the same goes a long way.

When you are exhausted, the thing you are most likely to reveal is not Spirit, but the Robot. This is why it is so important to nurture Spirit, and to set up your life so that you are not always victimized by your job and your children. You need time for yourself, time to be alone and get your own needs satisfied.

It's also important to watch how you relate to your children, so that they aren't forced to take the place of your spouse or your therapist. Irene is a single parent who wants to spend as much time as she can with her children, so she doesn't date much. That was her choice and she was happy with it, but at one point she discovered that she had turned her oldest daughter into her only confidant. She would come home from work and dump everything on this daughter, because she had no other place to put it. Irene had to start developing closer relationships with her adult friends so that her daughter wouldn't be forced into this position. I'm not suggesting that you can't tell your kids you've had a hard day at work, but that is different from unloading everything on them in the name of intimacy.

Another danger is developing a relationship in which the child takes on the role of "spouse." When Jeff came to see me at the age of twenty-three, he was still trying to extricate himself from an unhealthy relationship with his mother. He had been her companion and confidant for nearly twenty years. From the age of five he had been dressed up in suits and ties and accompanied her out to dinner, to parties, to the theater. And he had always felt so proud when she called him "her little man." But now he wanted out and he was terrified. Perhaps she could kill herself, or stop speaking to him (one of the methods she had often used as a control), or recount all she had done for him. His guilt almost won out. But eventually Jeff made the break. Fortunately, his mother remarried. Jeff finally was able to establish a healthy relationship with someone who not only loved him but could also support him in standing up to his mother.

We've already talked about not making the people at work your family, so where do you put your feelings, your upsets? I think it is very important for single parents to have support groups and activities outside the home. I know this is difficult because there are already so many demands on your time and you want to spend as much of it as possible with the kids. To this I say, *do it anyway!* You have to do it for yourself or you may be in serious trouble, and in the end it will serve your children. It doesn't have to cost much. There are church groups, Al-Anon, Adult Children of Alcoholics, Parents Without Partners, and many other groups that cost virtually nothing. Find a place where you can dump your Robot stuff so you can be intimate with your family.

Your children also need support outside the family. Being children, they are going to be involved with their Robots a lot of the time. You may not want, or be able, to handle all this Robot-like behavior, especially if you are trying to avoid slipping into your own Robot. Find a place where their

Robots can dump, too, so that they don't have to bring it all home, either. There are many children's support groups, and it may be enough for them just to be involved in after-school activities or sports. Running around screaming on a basketball court or hockey field for a couple hours after school does wonders.

It's also important for kids to have friends outside the home to avoid the kind of exclusivity and isolation that can build up in single-parent families. As in Jeff's situation, when the parent and child become "best friends," sometimes the child is reluctant to develop normal social contacts for fear of "betraying" the parent—especially if the parent has "given up everything for them" and is unconsciously projecting his or her loneliness. The child can begin to feel guilty and obliged to spend excessive amounts of time with the parent.

Children in a single-parent family need to know that there are a lot of demands on their parent's time and energy, and that they need to help out. They can't start thinking of their parent as a slave whose job it is to earn all the money, cook all the meals, keep the house clean, make their Halloween costumes, and then tuck them into bed each night with a smile. They need to participate emotionally, and they also need to help with the chores. Even little children can fold laundry and dust, and these jobs can be turned into fun the family shares.

The single parents I know have found it very helpful to develop contacts with other single parents—either as friends or as housemates. It's becoming quite common for two single parents of the same or opposite sex to combine households. You might have to learn to adjust to the other person's style, and your children might learn some new ways of doing things, but these kinds of friendships and living situations can make everyone's life easier.

Again, the same dynamics are at work here as in traditional families, but in more extreme forms. The exaggeration in single-parent families usually has to do with exhaustion, and occasionally with an overly close bonding between parent and child. When you are aware of these stumbling blocks, it's easier to avoid them.

4. *Families With Two Working Parents.* This situation is similar to the single-parent family. There is a lot of exhaustion in the air. Both parents work hard and then come home to cooking, cleaning, and children. There isn't a lot of time for relaxed, spontaneous family activities, for just hanging out and being together. Parents aren't always available to their children, and children have to learn to deal with that.

Mothers are apt to be particularly tired. Women's roles may be changing, but mother still does most of the shopping, cooking, and cleaning even if she works the same number of hours as her husband. It's important for women to know what they do and do not want to do, and to be able to communicate it. The alternative is holding down two full-time jobs—one at the office and one at home.

One of the greatest challenges in a home with two working parents is finding time just to have fun together. Schedules are tight, everybody is busy, and people aren't always free at the same time. Even if you have to schedule family outings and events far in advance, it's important to do so. There have been many times in history when families haven't had a lot of free time together, when everyone was working in factories or on farms twelve hours a day. The trick is to celebrate the time you do have together and to make fun out of activities like getting dinner, doing the dishes, washing the car, or cleaning the house. This is another reason it's important for children to help with these activities. A lot of quality communication and interaction can happen during these times. Problems can be worked out, lives can be shared, and intimacy can take place.

Child care is another issue for families with single and two working parents. We used to have extended families in which there was always a grandma or a maiden aunt at home to take care of the children. Now those grandmas and maiden aunts are traveling the world or involved in the senior center or holding down a job, and we might not want them to come live with us even if they were available. Many types of child care are available, depending on the ages of your children. The important thing is that you feel good about where they are and what they are doing. Connecting with other parents and sharing child care is often the most cost-effective way of handling this issue.

One of the lessons of being in this type of family is learning to take care of yourself. Spend some time alone looking at your own needs. You have responsibilities to your family, but you also have a responsibility to yourself. Make sure your own needs are met, and that you are doing the things that are important to you. Maybe you need some time alone between the office and home. Instead of trying to crash through dinner as soon as you walk in the house, with everybody tense and tired, maybe you need to take fifteen minutes just to lie down with a cloth over your eyes and listen to quiet music. You may need some kind of break before you get into all the chaos. If that's the case, make your announcement and stick to it. You may encourage others to do the same.

5. *Families With an Illness.* When a family member is chronically or perhaps fatally ill, circumstances and reactions will vary according to the role the victim has played in the family, but certain factors will exist anytime the family is wounded in this way. These include denial, anger, fear, frustration, guilt, and dependence; all highly survival-oriented emotions which can block intimacy if not acknowledged and dealt with.

The most difficult to acknowledge, of course, is denial, because its purpose is to keep us from seeing what is happening for as long as possible. In these kinds of illnesses there is too much loss and pain for the Robot to bear.

Denial will be compounded if the illness is a "shameful" one, which might get the family ostracized, but it exists in any illness which involves loss of power. Denial is a coping mechanism which is initially helpful. It becomes a problem when it keeps the victim and family from facing the issue.

The sooner everyone can break through the denial, the sooner the family can begin to truly join forces and help each other through the experience. Usually, however, family members break through at different times and this can create havoc with intimacy.

When Jim was diagnosed as having colon cancer, Carol's denial came in the form of wanting to "do something about it" right away. Jim's came in the form of ignoring the whole thing. The more Carol wanted to talk about it, get more life insurance for Jim, pay the children's tuitions five years in advance, and get a job, the more Jim retreated into his shell. Carol thought she was facing the situation, and that Jim was in denial. Jim thought he was handling it very well and that Carol was hysterical. The kids couldn't figure out what was going on. Their mom was whirling about talking to doctors and weeping over the phone to her mom, and their dad was acting like nothing was wrong except he stayed away at work longer than ever before.

When Carol came to me she was panic-stricken, because she couldn't get Jim to "face the issue." As she began to explore what was going on, she could see that her Robot was in denial also. It was denying Carol the experiences of fear, frustration, dependence, anger, and guilt which she would be having if she stopped long enough to notice them.

Carol had some difficulty understanding why she should allow herself to have those feelings until she saw two things: first, that only by going through those feelings and dealing with them would she finally reach a state of acceptance, and second, that she was having those feelings anyway and they were running her life.

Once Carol was able to respond to her own feelings and stopped blaming Jim for them, Jim became more willing to open up to Carol about his fears. He never became as vocal as Carol would have liked, but he did begin to talk with her,

and as he and Carol talked, the children became less frightened of asking questions. They became intrigued by explanations of the treatments Jim was receiving and often
accompanied him to the doctor. The last I heard, the older
son had decided to become a physician as a result of the care
given Jim by a noted oncologist.

Jim's cancer is in remission right now. The family had
quite a scare. But as the result of their brush with death, they
have learned not to take each other for granted and to live
each day to the fullest. They have taken a situation which
could have seriously distanced them and used it to their
advantage.

If Your Family Is Dysfunctional

If your family is dysfunctional, then you need more help
than this book can give you. But how do you know if your
family is dysfunctional? A dysfunctional family cannot do its
job of supporting the individuals within the family in making
their contribution to society. Caught up in its fear of non-
survival, the family turns inward to protect itself, denies the
situation, and destructs. Feeding on its own pain, yet resisting
it mightily, the family implodes. There may be one or two
hardy survivors, but the family as a whole is destroyed.

Over and over again I see examples of this in my work.
One graphic case is that of Leanne. Her mother was an alcoholic from a wealthy and prominent San Francisco family,
her father a military man who could not afford to have an
alcoholic wife. Leanne and her sister grew up in an environment of secrecy, flare-ups, and threats, all of which were
covered up by a facade of protocol, opera openings, cotillions,
and private schools. Long before Leanne's mother died of
an alcohol-barbiturate overdose, the family had sickened and
died. Leanne's father had siphoned off most of his wife's
inheritance and divorced her. Leanne's sister had a nervous
breakdown. And Leanne, at age thirty-five, the apparent

"survivor," was wrestling mightily with issues of intimacy and relationships which were affecting not only her personal life but her career as well.

Even if your family seems to be functioning fine, but you're having difficulty, it's important to get professional help. Perhaps the denial in your family is so great that nobody but you can feel anything, much less recognize it as a problem to be dealt with.

In my work with alcoholics and their families I am repeatedly struck by the power of denial, the mechanism by which Robots avoid the most blatant truths in order to protect themselves from an unbearable experience.

When it comes to alcoholism and other addictions, it's important to realize that it is almost impossible to have true intimacy with an addict, because he has a relationship with the bottle or the drug that distorts his truth, and nothing can break through that until he is clean and sober. You may have to leave him in order to have the kind of relationship you want. Of course, if you choose to stay with him for religious or other reasons, you can create an intimate family for yourself outside of the relationship and get support in that way.

Before you give up, however, you might consider an intervention. In order to do this you must find a qualified counselor to assist you and the family in this process. Otherwise, you can cause more harm than good.

If you do choose to intervene, it must be from the perspective of communicating those things you need to reveal to the alcoholic which you have either suppressed or blurted out in an inappropriate way. Many people intervene with the intention of "forcing the alcoholic to quit drinking." This is a deadly agenda which can easily backfire. An intervention is a superb opportunity to let yourself be known. That should be your only purpose.

If there is no addiction in your family that you're aware of, there are plenty of other kinds of dysfunction. The important thing is to get professional help rather than try to figure it out yourself.

* * *

Special families have come together despite the odds,
and they have been drawn together by love. Intimacy is a
way of experiencing and expressing that love on an even
deeper level. Their special circumstances mean they need to
be more conscious of nurturing their relationships and creating intimacy, and so the opportunities are great.

QUESTIONS TO ASK YOURSELF

In what way is your family special?
How does that specialness block intimacy?
How does that specialness enhance intimacy?
How do you take care of yourself?
How much time do you have just for you?

THINGS TO DO

List the steps you need to take in order to take care of your-
    self.

CHAPTER NINE

CHOOSING INTIMACY

The Choice *Not* to Be Intimate

In order to choose intimacy, you have to have the option *not* to choose it. Some people will read this book and decide that they don't want anything to do with intimacy. They don't want to make themselves known, or listen while others make themselves known. They are happy alone, and they want to keep it that way.

Even if you *do* want intimacy in your life, there will be times when living on a desert island sounds like heaven. We all need to build some nonintimate time and space into our lives, time when we don't have to make ourselves known to anybody and don't have to listen to anybody make themselves known to us.

If you are a single parent with three children, no money, no baby-sitter, and a one-room studio, this is going to be difficult. *But you have to do it.* You won't be able to be a good parent unless you have some time for yourself. It's almost impossible to create the space for intimacy if you have to do it all the time. You will feel pressured, invaded, worn down, and burned out. You may have to "trade children" with some-one, taking their children for an afternoon and having them take your children in return, but you have to create some space for yourself.

The same is true if you are a married working parent. You have to find time for yourself, and also time for just yourself and your spouse. Even if it is only a half hour a week, make that half hour and take it all for yourself.

If intimacy is *not* your choice, be prepared for people to prod you, poke you, and try to force intimacy on you. People who want intimacy have a hard time believing that there are actually people who *don't* want it. They think you are hiding from something, or just disillusioned. They want the world to be one big, happy family. They will imply that there is something wrong with you and try to win you over to their point of view. They will introduce you to people and make snide remarks about your not having many friends, or say things like, "My, that computer seems to be your best friend."

I worked with a man, Joel, who, after taking a look at what was involved in true intimacy, decided that it just wasn't for him at that point in his life. It simply wasn't worth the risk and the pain. He lived alone, worked hard, and was highly successful. He enjoyed television and had a famous collection of model cars. He had been through all sorts of therapies and human potential groups, but intimacy just wasn't something he wanted.

Because I place a high value on intimacy, there are times when I wonder if he is really happy. On the other hand, when I get home from work and have fifteen phone calls to return to all my intimate friends and family, I sometimes envy him. I wouldn't trade my own choice, but I also have to let Joel have his. He has made himself known to me, and I have to respect his choice. He may not want to live that way forever, but for now, intimacy is not what he wants. The greatest service I can do him is to stop prodding and poking him and introducing him to nice women.

Even if Joel is kidding himself, and really *wants* me to

prod and poke him, he is probably better off if I don't fall for this ploy. If I try to change him and give him a lot of attention for not wanting to be intimate, he will have more reason to stay there. If I let him be, he will find out if nonintimacy is really what he wants.

Sometimes it's hard to know when to let people alone, especially if you are a parent. If your child starts withdrawing and pulling away from people in an exaggerated way, you can't always just leave him to his own devices. The Robots of children and especially teenagers, are very active. They are constantly trying out new behaviors and testing the results. Your child's withdrawal may simply be a part of this experimentation and disappear in a week if it doesn't produce many interesting results. On the other hand, he may need some special attention. If he won't talk to you about what is going on, he may benefit from some professional support. If you are really concerned, you at least need to make that concern known.

Your child needs room to be the way he is and to try out different behaviors, but you also have responsibilities as a parent. If your child has a fever or a broken leg, you make sure he gets medical treatment. If he is very bright but getting low grades in school, you check to see what the problem is. If some unusual or uncharacteristic behavior persists or starts becoming a problem, you need to get to the source of it.

You have the same responsibilities to your spouse. If you are married to someone who is generally outgoing, and he starts weaving a cocoon around himself and becoming isolated, you must find out what the problem is.

Letting people make their choice for nonintimacy applies more to the person you meet and start dating who makes it very clear to you that intimacy is not something he wants in his life. That doesn't mean you can't say to him that you feel otherwise, but it's neither fair nor productive to try and change him.

If you are the person who doesn't want to be intimate, give yourself permission to do that. You don't have to sign a pledge to live alone for the rest of your life. There may come a time when you do want intimacy, but now you don't. In six months, after you have truly given yourself permission and experienced living this way, you may change your mind. Or you may not. Keep flexible, keep choosing, and let yourself have your choices.

You may be an adult and want to establish intimacy for the first time with your parents, and they may want nothing to do with it. They may prefer to keep talking about the weather and not want to reveal anything about themselves to you. You have to let them have that choice. It doesn't mean you can't reveal yourself to them if you choose, but you can't blame them for not wanting to do the same.

You always have a choice about how intimate you want to be with people, and they have the same choice with you. Respect their choices and your own.

Why Choose Intimacy?

I believe we are at an evolutionary crossroads. The old ways of being "intimate," the old ways of relating within families, have been based mostly on Robot-like behavior. What we want now is something more attuned to Spirit. The old ways haven't worked very well, and we are now in the process of finding new ways of relating and being intimate with one another. We've evolved beyond the need simply to survive and defend ourselves, and we are ready for something more—something based on our deepest nature and truths, something that touches our hearts as well as our minds.

Ultimately, life moves toward establishing a relationship with ourselves and our higher power. When we truly know ourselves, we know that the higher power is within. In the end, we all discover that we are nothing more, and nothing less, than expressions of the higher power. Intimacy gives us the opportunity to experience that, because it is the process through which we come to know ourselves.

We all face daily choices about intimacy, whether or not we are aware of it. We can be intimate with our parents, children, or spouse, with the checker at the market, with our friends, with anyone we encounter. Or we can choose to limit intimacy with these people. It all depends on how much of ourselves we want to reveal at that particular moment, and how willing we are to let them reveal themselves.

The fact that you have read this book indicates that for you these choices are more conscious than they are for some people. However, everyone on earth wants some level of intimacy—at least with themselves. We are all human, and part of being human is wanting to discover ourselves, share ourselves, and connect with the higher power.

Is intimacy really worth all the trouble and discomfort? For me, it is. I have the most precious thing in life—an experience of my true self, the higher power within—and no matter what happens, I have people around me who support me 1,000 percent, and who give me the privilege of supporting them 1,000 percent.

Our family has had its share of trouble. We've had deaths, financial difficulties, and addictions. In 1982 a mudslide destroyed our new home and most of our possessions. The thing that has made all this not only bearable but inspirational is what it has brought forth in our family and friends. It sounds funny to say that having your home destroyed in a mudslide can have wonderful aspects, but the experience of support and love with our family and friends, with everyone pulling together and bringing forth the best parts of themselves, almost made it worth it.

But intimacy isn't something that you do to get through the mudslides of life. It's something that happens minute by minute out of your desire to know and love yourself and others, and to connect with your higher power. It is a constant adventure that keeps you out there on the edge every minute, every day.

There is really very little we can count on in life. We want to think our earth is solid and secure, but the people

who experienced the Mexico City earthquake don't necessarily believe that anymore. We want to think the seasons are
predictable, but those of us who survived the California
floods of 1982 know better. People die. Parents separate. And
life goes on, as unexpected and unpredictable as ever.

It saddens me to see people on television who have been
involved in disasters crying, "Why me?" I figure, "Why *not*
me?" I'm involved in life, and life is going to hand up whatever experiences allow me to grow and become more than I
thought I was. A power higher and wiser than I am knew
that I would grow by having hundreds of pounds of mud
dumped on my house. Sometimes people think of God as an
accountant, and believe that if they just have faith and live
right, then bad things won't happen to them. We know this
isn't true. I believe we are given whatever lessons we are
capable of handling at the moment, and that our only job is
to rise to the occasion and learn those lessons.

That is what makes life exciting and aligns us with the
purpose of living. Our higher power is here to give us all the
support we need, at the exact moment that we need it. That
is the only thing we really *can* count on in life.

Relationships can be just as unpredictable and mystifying
as life. Intimacy is not there to help us avoid upsets, or to
"fix" all the painful things that happen when human beings
interact. It is there to let us deal with those things in a way
that moves us beyond our Robots, and lets us make the evolutionary leap into Spirit that we are here to make.

Upsets will always occur. People will betray and hurt one
another. We don't always do it on purpose, but we do it. Or
rather, our Robots do it. As we live, we constantly learn what
we can count on to get us through those times, and that is
Spirit, our relationship with the higher power, our truest,
deepest nature. The way we gain access to Spirit is through
intimacy, through the risk of making ourselves known to
ourselves and to others, and extending ourselves so that others can do the same.

When we live in Spirit, love is all that exists. "Who we

are" is love. The uncomfortable process of peeling away layers of the Robot and "who we are not" is just the means to this end. When we love, we are expressing the God within and we want others to have the chance to do the same thing.

The desire we all have to live in the Spirit, to experience and express the God within, is the bottom line for everything we do. When we get upset with other people, we are really just upset that they are not manifesting their highest being and so we feel cheated. We forget that people need the chance to bring up, see, accept, and then let go of their Robots before they can reveal the Spirit. When we are consciously aware of this process, and of our tendency to react from the Robot to their Robot-like behavior, it all becomes a little easier. Each time we emerge from the Robot into Spirit, our connection with the higher power becomes deeper and the road back to our true selves becomes clearer.

The experience of intimacy is the experience of union —with ourselves, with other people, and with our higher power. We are already one with these things; it's just that we don't always remember or *experience* that union. The connection with Spirit is what makes that experience possible. That is all we really want from life, and all we are meant to do.

Amazingly enough, as each one of us experiences and expresses Spirit, that expression Radiates out and casts light around us. Who we are is reflected in every encounter, every relationship, everything we do. We are not going to change the world by changing things outside of ourselves. Only as we become known to ourselves will that state of being be reflected in our world. By learning to face ourselves, all our demons and all our gifts, we can learn to face our mirror, the Universe. Only then will we be able to truly respond to that which we have created. Peace, love, and understanding cannot exist as concepts or ideas. They must be an experience that we have within, for ourselves and for our fellowman. Loving the Russian people and hating the "regime" won't work. The regime is made up of people. Fighting for the underdog and despising the perpetrator won't work, either. The perpetrator is a human being also. Caring about the poor and resenting the rich is a useless exercise. The rich are people, too. Until we reconcile all these aspects of ourselves, they will be reflected back to us as reminders of our unwillingness to face the truth. We are human beings. We contain Spirit, but we also contain Robot. If we truly want peace on earth, we must come to terms with ourselves, Robot and all. Resistance only creates persistence. The volume will only get louder unless we are willing to hear the truth. Creating intimacy is the first step in the process.

Intimacy is a state of being. It is the state of being on the path. The path leads to an experience of the God within which allows the God within to be expressed. We each approach intimacy in our own way, and find our own path to the higher power. Intimacy has opened up worlds for me that I never knew existed. I hope it will do the same for you.

INDEX

A

Acceptance
  of biological family, 126–127
  and love, 8–9
Addiction
  co-addict, role of, 81
  and family life, 163–164, 176–177
  to nonintimate communication,
    81–84
  and "Robot" self, 21–22
Adult Children of Alcoholics, 127,
    130, 164
Al-Anon, 107, 127, 130
Alcoholism, 79, 92
  denial of, 83–84
  and intimacy, 177
Anger
  dumping, 85–86
  guidelines for dealing with, 86
  suppression of, 85

B

Birth order, and family roles, 39–40,
    41–46

Blame, 18
  in dysfunctional family, 56–57

C

Charmer, child's role in family, 45–46
Children's roles
  charmer, 45–46
  loner, 44–45
  perfect child, 41–43
  rebel, 43–44
Choices, and intimacy, 69–70
Co-addict, role of, 81
Communication
  barrier to, 78–79
  definition of, 20
  genetic factors, 8
  nonintimate communication,
    addiction to, 81–84
  and "Robot" self, 78–79, 84–87
  and self-knowledge, 79–80
  and "Spirit" self, 80
  See also Intimate communication.
Control, and "Robot" self, 26
Coping, meaning of, 91

Criticism
  in family relationships, 71–72
  and "Robot" self, 25–26

D

Defensiveness, and "Robot" self, 22–
  23, 26
Denial, alcoholism, 83–84
Dual earner families, 173–174
Dumping, and communication, Robot
  self, 85–87
Dysfunctional family, 54–60, 124
  addicted families, 163–164, 176–177
  blame in, 56–57
  case example, 55–57
  causes of, 54–55
  guidelines for, 59
  members' impairments, 58
  perspective of, 58
  and "Robot" self, 56–58
  signs of dysfunction, 176

E

Emotional impairment, in
      dysfunctional family, 58
Expectations
  barrier to intimacy, 95–101
  and disappointment, 98
  intimacy and family, 125–126
  parent-child relationship, 100–101
  and "Robot" self, 95–97, 99

F

Families
  acceptance of biological family, 126–
      127
  changes in structure, 20–21
  common bonds, capitalizing on,
      128–129
  definition of, 37
  highest purpose of, 29–30
  historical perspective, 34–35
  "perfect family," 34–37
  special situations
      dual earner families, 173–174
      gay families, 168–170
      illness in family, 174–176
      single-parent families, 170–173
      step families, 164–168
  supportiveness of, 29–30
  See also Family roles; New family,
      creating.
Family council, 130

Family roles, 39–50
  and birth order, 39–40
  case example, 48–50
  charmer, 45–46
  clinging to, 107–109
  father, 40
  homeostasis, 50–53
  loner, 44–45
  mother, 40–41
  perfect child, 41–43
  rebel, 43–44
  scapegoating, 47
  single-parent family, 171
  turn-taking and, 39
Father, role of, 40
Fear, of loss, 101–102
Forgiveness, self and others, 18
Friendship, intimacy and, 20

G

Gay families, 168–170
Genetic factors, communication, 8

H

Hidden agendas
  and communication, 88–89
  "Robot" self, 88–89
Higher Power
  connecting to, 19–20
  and "Spirit" self, 24
Homeostasis, family, 50–53, 124

I

Illness in family, 174–176
Intimacy
  barriers to
      clinging to past, 106–110
      earning love, 117–118
      expectations, 95–101
      fear of loss, 101–102
      need to be needed, 115–117
      never getting enough, 113–115
      others doing less, 118–120
      perception of non-communication,
          120–121
      resentments, 110–112
      "Robot" self, 103–105
      trying to change another, 112–113
  choice and, 61–63
  and connection to higher power,
      19–20
  definition of, 11
  versus expression of opinion, 12

forced on others, 63–64
and friendship, 20
as natural state, 4, 19–20, 72
non-intimacy, choice for, 180–182
reasons for, 183–186
and "Robot" self, 20–23, 25–27,
    28–29
sex differences, 8
sex mistaken with, 10–11
and "Spirit" self, 23–25, 26, 29, 30
steps toward, 64–68
    first step, 67–68
    making choices, 70
    self-acceptance, 65–67
    unblocking barriers, 70–74
uncomfortable aspects of, 74
and vulnerability, 17–18
Intimacy and family
choices in, 125–131
guidelines for, 131–141
    clearing slate, 131–137, 152–153
    constancy of communication, 140
    constancy of intimacy, 139
    description versus evaluation in
        communication, 140
    direct communication, 138
    encouragement of others, 139–140
    hearing truth, 137–138
    truth-telling, 137
lack of, case example, 5–7, 12–17
time as problem, 7
Intimate communication
and emotions, 87
and hidden agendas, 88–89
and moccasin walking, 90–91
outside resources as help for, 91–93
and self-communication, 88, 89

L

Labeling, 92
Loner, child's role in family, 44–45
Loss, fear of, 101–102
Love
and acceptance, 8–9
misconceptions about, 117–118

M

Materialism, 113–114
Mother, role of, 40–41

N

Need
    need to be needed, 115–117
    and relationship, 69

New family (creating)
choosing right people, 149–150
efforts in, 147–149
guidelines for, 150–157
reasons for, 145–146
rewards of, 161

P

Parent-child relationship
expectations, 100–101
need in, 69
Past
    clearing slate, family, 131–137, 152–153
    clinging to, as barrier to intimacy,
        106–110
    and "Robot" self, 22
Payoffs, and communication, 88
Perfect child, child's role in family,
    41–43
Points of view, moccasin walking and,
    90–91
Professional help, use of, 91–93, 130–131

R

Rationalization, and "Robot" self, 27
Reactions, of "Robot" self, 20–21
Rebel, child's role in family, 43–44
Relationships
common conceptions about, 9–10
need in, 69
and self-esteem, 114
Resentment, as barrier to
    communication, 110–112
"Robot" self, 20–23, 25–27, 28–29
and addiction, 21–22
as barrier to intimacy, 103–105
and communication, 78–79
    dumping in, 85–87
    hidden agendas, 88–89
    payoffs, 88
    stuffing in, 84–85
and criticism, 25–26
defensiveness of, 22–23, 26
in dysfunctional family, 56–58
example of, 23
expectations of, 95–97, 99
facade of, 26
intimacy, blocking of, 27–28
and past experiences, 22
and rationalization, 27
reactivity of, 20–21
recognition of, 24–25, 29

S

Self-acceptance, and intimacy, 65–67
Self-esteem, and relationships, 114
Self-knowledge, and communication, 79–80
Sensitivity, person's "hot spots," 9–10
Sex, intimacy mistaken for, 10–11
Sex differences, meaning of intimacy, 8
Single-parent families, 170–173
Spirit self
   and communication, 80
   conscious choice about, 24–25
   and higher power, 24
   love and, 184–185
   nourishment of, 30
   perception of others from, 29

Step families, 164–168
Stuffing, and communication, Robot self, 84–85

T

Trust, basis of, 18

V

Vulnerability, and intimacy, 17–18

W

Workplace
   co-workers, relationships with, 159–160
   survival issues, 158, 159